BUILD A
DOLL'S HOUSE

BUILD A
DOLL'S HOUSE

MICHAL MORSE

KALMBACH BOOKS

This book is dedicated to Laura Bishop, whose life has been transformed by the gift of a doll's house through the Children's Wish Foundation.

Photographs by John Drysdale
Front cover photograph by Trevor Hurst
Plans by George Buchanan
Other illustrations and location photographs by the author
Doll's houses built by Trevor and Sue Cook

First published 1992, reprinted 1993

© Michal Morse 1992

Typeset by Tek-Art Ltd, West Wickham, Kent and printed in Hong Kong

Published by
B.T. Batsford Ltd
4 Fitzhardinge Street
London W1H 0AH

A catalogue record for this book is available from the British Library

ISBN 0-89024-188-0

Library of Congress Cataloging-in-Publication Data

Morse, Michal.
    Build a doll's house / by Michal Morse.
        p.   cm.
    Originally published: London : B.T. Batsford, 1992
    Includes index.
    ISBN 0-89024-188-0 ; $19.95
    1. Dollhouses.   I. Title.
TT175.3.M6/   1993
745.592'3--dc20   93-25460
                        CIP

CONTENTS

ACKNOWLEDGEMENTS

My grateful thanks go to Trevor and Sue Cook, who have translated my designs so perfectly into three-dimensional reality; Barbara Warner for her invaluable advice on wiring; all my friends among the collectors and craftsmen for their helpful advice; Faith Eaton for all her help and encouragement; and my marvellous staff at The Dolls House in Covent Garden, London, who have allowed me time off to write this book.

A doll's house really comes to life once it is furnished – the dressing table set, a mixing bowl, and the flowers on the table all help to create a special miniature household

INTRODUCTION

This book is intended to encourage doll's house enthusiasts of all ages to build their ideal house.

When I opened The Dolls House in 1971, it was the first specialist shop of its kind in England. Since then, I must have sold thousands of doll's houses in a variety of styles, particularly since moving to Covent Garden, London, in 1980. Many customers have asked for plans of the designs we sell, so I have finally decided to work out a basic four-room house that can be adapted to different styles, and have included tips I have picked up from craftsmen over the years.

Originally rich women's toys in the seventeenth and eighteenth centuries, doll's houses were mass-produced for children in the late nineteenth and the twentieth centuries. Now, once again, they are collected by adults as well as children, and the whole family can enjoy them. For some women, a doll's house can be a dream house, the country cottage she will never live in, and for once she can have full control over decoration and furnishing. One collector startled her family by discussing re-decorating the dining room, when it was the one in the doll's house she meant!

Some people think us eccentric. I remember an aunt being most amused by my (real-life) sitting room, which she thought was like a big nursery. I was so used to other collectors' homes that I had forgotten most people do *not* have a large rocking horse, antique brass trains and a Victorian doll's house in the room where they entertain their friends.

Doll's houses are still thought of as being primarily for children. The designs in this book can be adapted for any age. A simple four-room house can be a child's plaything or, with added detail, an adult's miniature country retreat. Given the same basic structure, the windows and stairs can be varied and the exterior painted a flat colour, or to simulate brick, flint, stone or Tudor studwork. The basic house shape is very familiar, the first building a child learns to draw.

For something more ambitious, a six-room Georgian-style house is the most popular. It has an elegant façade and a comfortable number of rooms to furnish – a kitchen and dining room on the ground floor, a sitting room and bedroom, and a choice between nursery, bathroom, study or music room. An enthusiastic collector can add more detail to the staircase, and alter the front to Regency or Victorian.

If you are short of space, the small shop can stand on a table or hang on a wall. (I have even seen miniature rooms set into a wall, and the riser of a staircase.)

Decorating is fun, and there are tips on how to choose colour schemes and fit the mouldings. If you want to light your house, the different methods, using tape and wire, are explained. When you come to choosing the furniture, there is a wide range available from specialist shops – mass-produced furniture from Taiwan, kits from America, and a fine selection from skilled British craftsmen. Their scale is 1 in : 1 ft (the scale I use in this book), larger than most toyshop furniture which is ¾ in : 1 ft. This means that a chair seat should be 1½ in (1½ ft) from the ground, and the top surface of a table 2½ in (2½ ft) from the ground. The houses must have doors at least 6 in (6 ft) high and ceilings cannot be less than 7 in (7 ft). Once you know the scale, it is easy to recognize what will fit. You will learn to adapt household items for small-scale use – lace glass mats make good tablecloths, for instance.

If you feel inspired to make your own design, perhaps a copy of your own house, there are tips on how to plan it and instructions for different staircases and windows. You will find this a very infectious hobby. Doll's houses appeal to everybody, so all your friends will want one, too!

THE FOUR-ROOM HOUSE

I have chosen to build a detached cottage, with overhanging roof, because it is difficult to find this design ready-made. Four rooms make a good basic shape to start with: two up and two down, central staircase, size 26 in (66 cm) wide x 26 in (66 cm) high x 12 in (30.5 cm) deep. The house may be painted (I find brick paper wears badly), detailed to simulate brick or flint, or covered in 'weatherboard'. The scale is 1 in : 1 ft (i.e. 1/12th).

The roof may be plain grey, tiled with card, plywood, lino or even pottery tiles, or thatched. Embossed sheets of tiles, slates and bricks are also available.

Once you have built one house, you can create a whole village of different designs by simply altering the exteriors. You can start with the BASIC HOUSE, which has one flight of simple block stairs and plain windows.

The BRICK HOUSE is painted and scored to simulate brick. The roof has card strips of 'slate', dormer windows, a lift-off front roof for access, and a chimney on the back slope. The return staircase has two short flights, a half-landing and banisters.

The WEATHERBOARD HOUSE, based on Kent cottages, has wider windows, set close to the eaves, a simple door frame and lintel set straight in the line of the weatherboard.

The FLINT HOUSE is a more ambitious project, with detailed painting of brick and flint, arched windows, decorative ridge tiles and porch, and a slightly taller chimney.

The TUDOR HOUSE has a steeper roof than those of a later period, said to help snow slide off the thatch, so the roof panels are slightly deeper and need to be planed or cut to fit at the ridge. The 'leaded' windows are set as close as possible to the eaves. The large brick chimney has an inglenook fireplace, and the roof is thatched. Tiles would also be in period, but not grey slate, which is typically Victorian. The block stairs are used in this house.

The general instructions which follow describe the construction of the basic four-room house from which all the others are adapted, with individual details in the appropriate chapters.

What you will need

Tools

Cross-cut saw, electric jigsaw or circular saw, for cutting up panels of plywood
Padsaw, or jigsaw, for cutting out windows
Stanley knife, for cutting thin strips of wood; an additional saw blade attachment is useful
Craft knife, with assorted blades
Small backsaw and mitre block, for cutting strip wood at angles
Small drill and 3/64 in (1 mm) bit, for piloting panel pins
Drill and bit, for starting window openings
Small vice
G-clamps
Small hammer and pin punch
Small screwdriver, to scribe bricks
Bradawl, for starting holes
T-square and set square
Pencil and graph paper
Black biro, for marking floorboards
Metal ruler, or straight edge
Soldering iron, and core solder, for lighting
Side cutters or pliers, for cutting short doorknobs or screws
Hacksaw and lubricating oil, for cutting piano hinges
Paintbrushes and small paint roller

Materials

8 ft x 4 ft (224 cm x 122 cm) sheet of 3/8 in (9 mm) Finnish birch ply or medium-density fibreboard (harder to saw but does not split at cut edges)
Small sheets and strips of modelmaker's wood (obeche, spruce or pine), available in various thicknesses, for doors, windows and simple mouldings
Small sheets of thin plywood, to cut to size and use in the same way
1 in (2.5 cm) panel pins

Starting with one design, you can alter the exterior to create five quite different houses – BASIC, BRICK, WEATHERBOARD, FLINT and TUDOR

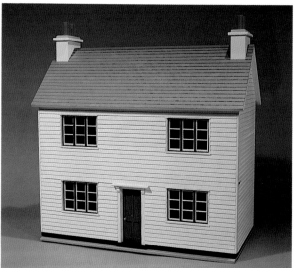

White PVA wood glue, for most joints
Contact adhesive, for quicker setting
Two-part epoxy resin (Araldite), for small tricky joints
Instant glue (Loctite Super Glue 3), for doorknobs and lights
Wood filler
Acrylic primer
Sandpaper, in various grades
Masking tape
Wallpaper and paste
Perspex or plastic, for windows
Hinges – cranked, flush or piano
Brass countersunk screws, for hinges
Triangle section, for roof edges and Return Staircase
Birdmouth or square angle, for the roof ridge
Card, for tiles and slates
Silk vinyl emulsion, for decorating inside and outside
Coloured varnish, for floors
Softwood, for block stairs and chimneys
Dowel, for chimney pots
Brass hook and eye, for side fastening
Copper tape or fine wire, for lighting

Further details of tools and materials are given in the instructions for each house.

Note
Initial capital letters are used throughout the book to refer to the cut panels of wood that appear on the cutting plans (see pages 12, 13, 61 and 81).

Unfamiliar architechural terms can be found in the Glossary on page 105.

Planning

Draw the plans on your sheet of plywood. Allow $1/16$ in (1.5 mm) between the pencil lines for the sawcut. The cutting diagram (Fig 1) shows the most economical way to cut out. If you cannot transport such a large sheet, most wood merchants will cut to size. (N.B. The cutting plan for the TUDOR HOUSE (Fig 2) gives a taller roof and side panels, to make an angle at the ridge sharper than the usual 90°.) Use good-quality wood, and make sure before cutting that it is flat and not warped. Do not rely on the sheet being exactly square; if you do not have a large T-square and set square, you can check by measuring opposite diagonals as you draw out the panels.

The Internal Floor of the BASIC HOUSE and TUDOR HOUSE has to be cut into two floors, each $10\frac{1}{2}$ in wide x 12 in deep (26.7 cm x 30.5 cm), but it is best to assemble the block stairs first and check the space left between the Internal Walls and Sides before cutting the exact width.

Draw windows and doorways on the cut panels, making sure any blemishes in the wood are kept on the inside (Fig 3). For the return staircase, mark the cut-out for the stairwell in the Floor, and the slot in the Internal Walls. If you are using the simple block stairs, remember the doorways on the top floor are at the back of the house; the centre window has to be narrower than the other windows to fit this hallway. Indicate the position of the dormer windows and trapdoor on the Front Roof and Top of the BRICK HOUSE, and the inglenook fireplace and the window on the Sides of the TUDOR HOUSE. The WEATHERBOARD HOUSE has no central window, so if you wish to light the staircase mark a window in the Back.

8 ft x 4 ft   ⅜ in birch ply

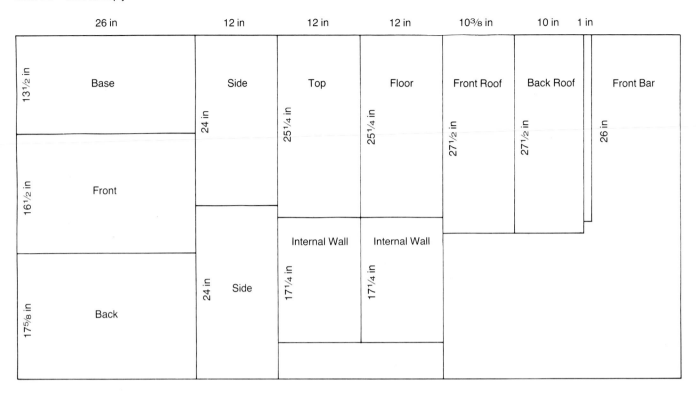

Fig 1 Cutting diagram – standard four-room house

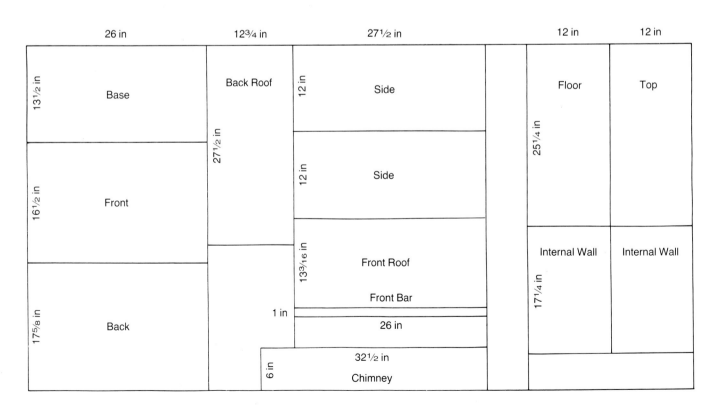

Fig 2 Cutting diagram – TUDOR HOUSE

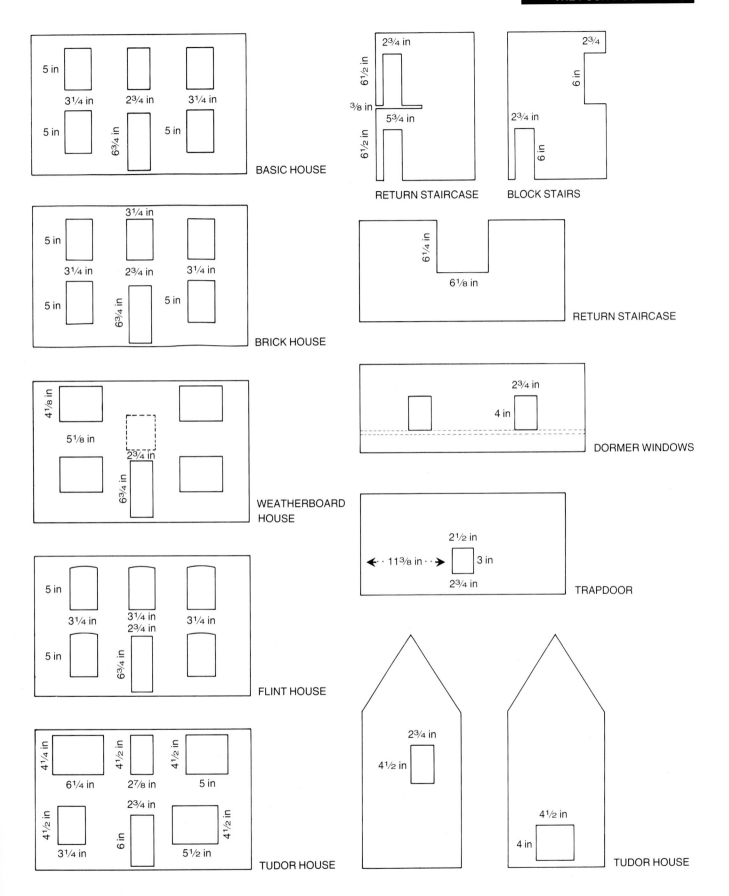

Fig 3 Cutting diagram – doors and windows

Cutting

To cut gable ends off the Sides, measure 6 in (15.2 cm) down, rule a guideline from the centre top to each side and cut off the two corners (Fig 4). For the TUDOR HOUSE, measure 9¼ in (23.5 cm) down (Fig 5) on the Side panels, which are 27½ in (69.9 cm) instead of the standard 24 in (61 cm) high. Cut away to the centre top as before, leaving a much sharper angle at the ridge.

To cut out the windows and front door, first drill near one corner. You may need two or three consecutive holes before inserting the jigsaw, or padsaw, unless you have a large drill bit. Cut along the ruled line to the

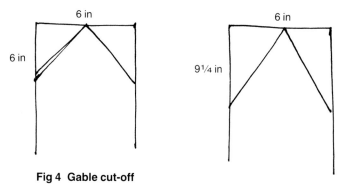

Fig 4 Gable cut-off

Fig 5 Tudor gable

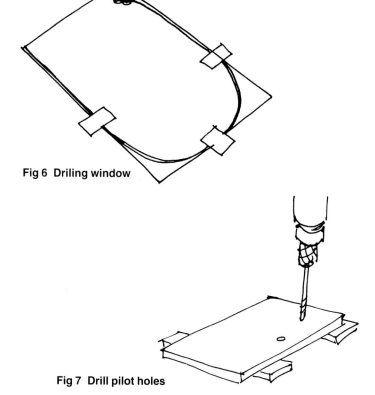

Fig 6 Driling window

Fig 7 Drill pilot holes

next corner (Fig 6). Remove the saw, return to about 1 in (2.5 cm) from the corner and cut a curve to the next side. Repeat until the centre wood is loose, then tape in position while cutting back to the other three corners – the wood will keep the blade upright. Clean up the corners once the scrap is removed. If you do not have a workbench, you can use a low table or firm stool, holding the wood steady with your left hand and knee.

The slots for the Floor with the return staircase may need trimming with a chisel. Cut the trapdoor in the Top of the BRICK HOUSE, the inglenook and the window in the Sides of the TUDOR HOUSE, and the Back window in the WEATHERBOARD HOUSE.

Preparation

All the cut edges should be smoothed down, using fine sandpaper wrapped round a block of wood approximately 4 in x 2 in (10.2 cm x 5.1 cm). Any blemishes in the surface should be filled with wood filler and rubbed down when hardened, using a circular movement.

Floors should be ruled and varnished before assembly. (This prevents any paintmarks later.) Rule lines ½ in (12 mm) apart with a black biro, or similar pen, along the floor sections to simulate floorboards. Stain and varnish, or seal with two coats of acrylic satin finish Georgian Oak varnish, rubbed down between coats.

Paint all other surfaces with acrylic primer (which dries in two hours) and sand smooth. Remember to leave the part of the Base unvarnished where it extends beyond the Front. You can paint or paper the walls, being very careful not to cover the primer where the joints are to be glued. The hall should be decorated before the stairs are fitted.

Using a ³⁄₆₄ in (1 mm) drill bit, make pilot holes at the joints, about 4 in (10 cm) apart, and ³⁄₁₆ in (5 mm) from the edge, to prevent the panel pins splitting the wood. Where possible, drill from the surface to be glued, so that even if it is not quite vertical the panel pin will not miss the centre of the ³⁄₈ in (9 mm) panel edge. While drilling, raise the panel on two pieces of scrap wood, so the drill can go right through (Fig 7). If you prefer to use screws, drill pilot holes from the exterior, using a ⅛ in (3 mm) drill bit, and recess with a countersink bit for ¾ in (19 mm) no. 4 brass screws. (You could also use a bradawl.)

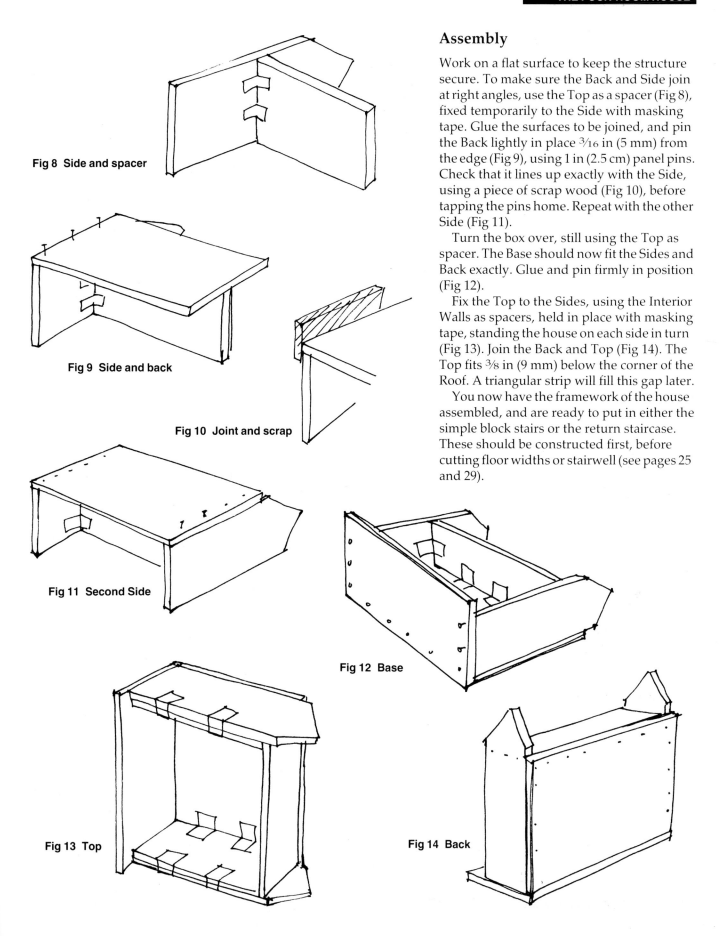

Fig 8 Side and spacer

Fig 9 Side and back

Fig 10 Joint and scrap

Fig 11 Second Side

Fig 12 Base

Fig 13 Top

Fig 14 Back

Assembly

Work on a flat surface to keep the structure secure. To make sure the Back and Side join at right angles, use the Top as a spacer (Fig 8), fixed temporarily to the Side with masking tape. Glue the surfaces to be joined, and pin the Back lightly in place 3/16 in (5 mm) from the edge (Fig 9), using 1 in (2.5 cm) panel pins. Check that it lines up exactly with the Side, using a piece of scrap wood (Fig 10), before tapping the pins home. Repeat with the other Side (Fig 11).

Turn the box over, still using the Top as spacer. The Base should now fit the Sides and Back exactly. Glue and pin firmly in position (Fig 12).

Fix the Top to the Sides, using the Interior Walls as spacers, held in place with masking tape, standing the house on each side in turn (Fig 13). Join the Back and Top (Fig 14). The Top fits 3/8 in (9 mm) below the corner of the Roof. A triangular strip will fill this gap later.

You now have the framework of the house assembled, and are ready to put in either the simple block stairs or the return staircase. These should be constructed first, before cutting floor widths or stairwell (see pages 25 and 29).

To fit the block stairs (BASIC and TUDOR HOUSES)

Check the width of the staircase against the Interior Walls before cutting the Floor into two sections, in case any adjustment is needed to the 10½ in (26.7 cm) width.

Pin and glue the Floors to the Interior Walls. Position by drawing the ceiling height 8⅝ in (21.9 cm) from the base. Tape together as shown (Fig 15), then brace the two constructions against each other (Fig 16) or use scrap (Fig 17). Be sure you make a lefthand and righthand Wall.

Secure the Walls to the Top and Back, using spacers the same length as the Floor (10½ in/26.7 cm) and ceiling height (8⅝ in/21.9 cm and 8¼ in/21 cm). Secure the Floors to the Sides and Back (Fig 18).

Lay the house on its Back and fix the Base to the Walls.

Glue the block stairs between the Interior Walls. The landing will be one step below the doorways. See page 25 for fitting the doors.

To fit the return staircase (BRICK, WEATHERBOARD and FLINT HOUSES)

If you are building the stairs first, check they fit in the 5⅜ in (13.7 cm) stairwell. Try fitting the Interior Walls and Floor. Glue all the edges to be joined. Pin the Top and Base to the Interior Walls, using scrap spacers 9⁹⁄₁₆ in (24.3 cm), the same as the room width. Position the Floor, using spacers as before (Fig 19). Pin through the doorway into the Wall below (Fig 20).

Fit the stairs into the stairwell and mark their position on the Walls. Fix the landing, then decorate before gluing the staircase in place (see page 29).

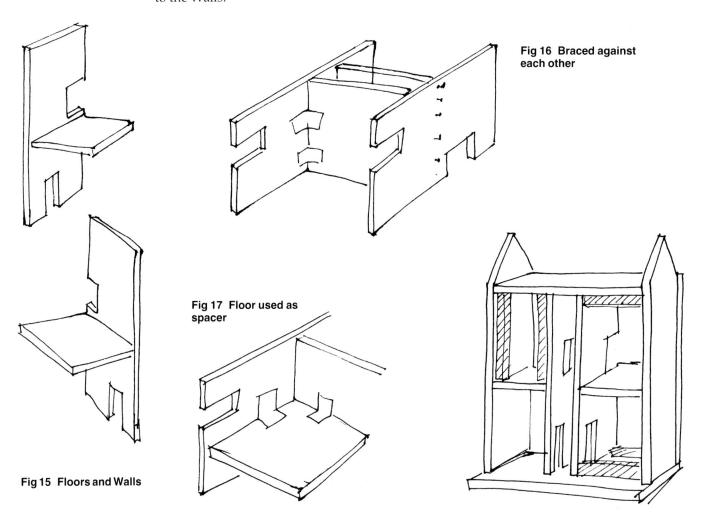

Fig 16 Braced against each other

Fig 17 Floor used as spacer

Fig 15 Floors and Walls

Fig 18 Block Stairs – walls and spacers

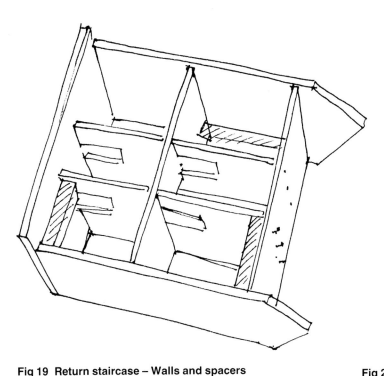

Fig 19 Return staircase – Walls and spacers

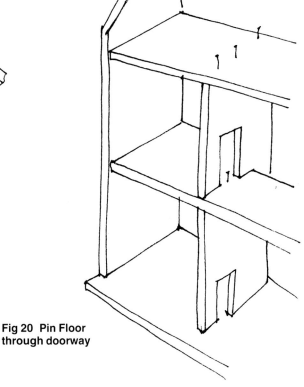

Fig 20 Pin Floor through doorway

Roof

Now that the main structure is firmly fitted together, braced by the staircase, the Roof can be fitted.

Glue and pin the Front Bar (Fig 21) level with the Top surface, after checking that the Front fits below. Cut two 26 in (66.1 cm) lengths of ⅜ in (9 mm) triangle, drill and pin along the top of the Front Bar and Back (Fig 22). This will fill the gap under the fixed Roof.

Opening roof (BRICK HOUSE)

This needs a larger triangle to act as a stop to keep the Roof on, one 26 in (66.1 cm) length of ¾ in (1.9 cm). Cut a ⅜ in (9 mm) notch out of each end, to fit within the Sides. See page 33 for further details.

Standard roof

Glue and pin the Back Roof, lining up by using scrap pinned on the front slope of the Sides (Fig 23). Fit the Front Roof in the same way, then glue and pin along the ridge.

Note: If the sides are to be painted in detail (brick or flint), you may prefer to fix the Roof later.

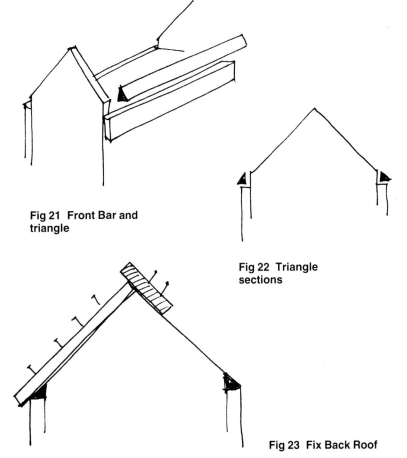

Fig 21 Front Bar and triangle

Fig 22 Triangle sections

Fig 23 Fix Back Roof

Chimney (BASIC and WEATHERBOARD HOUSES)
It is easier to make this in two sections than to cut a 'V' from one solid piece of wood. Cut 3½ in (8.9 cm) off a length of 2 in (5.1 cm) square-planed soft wood at a 45° angle in a mitre block. Cut a second piece to match (Fig 24). Glue them together under pressure, securing with masking tape. Bevel the top edge with a chisel, or round off with sandpaper. Repeat for the second chimney. Cut four chimney pots, 2 in (5.1 cm) long, from ¾ in (19 mm) birch dowel. Mark out the centre of each block by drawing diagonals, and make pilot holes with an awl. Drill the stack with a ¾ in (19 mm) bit if available, or use a small dowel as a peg, drilling into the pot as well (Fig 25).

Finish the stack by trimming with ⅜ in (9 mm) square, glued ⅜ in (9 mm) from the top (Fig 26). The BRICK and FLINT HOUSE chimneys have two layers of ⅛ in (3 mm), to correspond to the brick courses (Fig 27). The FLINT HOUSE has a taller chimney, 4¾ in (12 cm), to raise it above the decorative ridge tiles (see page 45). The BRICK HOUSE chimney fits on the Back Roof at a 45° angle (see page 34).

To position the chimney on the ridge, line it up with the Side (Fig 28). Glue and pin in position before fitting the chimney pots. Weight until dry, then add the pots. Cut birdmouth angle to fit between the stacks and to trim the ends of the ridge. Glue in position (Fig 29), unless you are adding tiles first (see page 36).

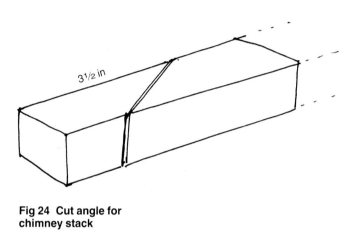

Fig 24 Cut angle for chimney stack

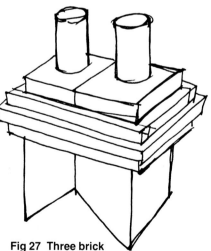

Fig 25 Peg chimney pots

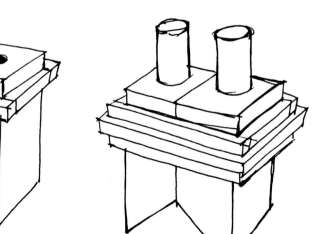

Fig 26 Brick course round stack

Fig 27 Three brick courses

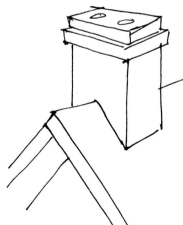

Fig 28 Fit chimney

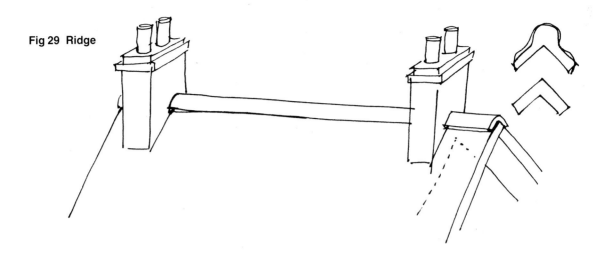

Fig 29 Ridge

Front

This should have been checked for fit when the Front Bar was fixed along the Top front. Choose which façade you want, noting that the BASIC HOUSE has a narrower centre window to fit within the hall of the block stairs. If you are using the return staircase (two flights), all the windows can be the same width, as in the BRICK HOUSE. The curved top of the FLINT HOUSE window has a radius of 7 in (18 cm) (see Fig 33 overleaf).

Fit the hinges first, to avoid damaging the Front when it is decorated. It can be detached later for any detailed work. Cranked cabinet hinges fit flat and are the easiest to fit. Use $7/16$ in (11 mm) hinges with $1/4$ in (6 mm) no. 4 brass countersunk screws. If you use butt hinges, remember to recess them into the Side Wall approximately $1/8$ in (3 mm), otherwise the hinged side of the Front will stand away from the house and not line up with the Front Bar.

Cranked hinges should be screwed to the inside of the Side Wall. Mark the edge of the Front where the hinges should come. Screw lightly in position, and check for fit until correct (Fig 30).

To fit butt hinges, cut a recess the full depth of the closed hinge in the front edge of the Side. Mark the screw positions by turning the hinge inside out, so it can fit the Side and edge at right angles (Fig 31). Mark screw holes on the inside Front in the same way. The Side will need thickening with $1/8$ in x $1/2$ in (3 mm x 12 mm) to fit a $1/2$ in (12 mm) hinge.

With the hinges firmly fixed to the Side, now screw them to the Front, adjusting for a correct fit. The Front should line up with the Sides, and hang level with the Base and Front Bar. To prevent the Front dropping and pulling on the hinges, a small wedge can be added at the foot of the other Side, so that the Front fits tightly (Fig 32). Make sure both sides of the Front are painted to avoid warping; keep it closed with a hook on the Side when the doll's house is not in use.

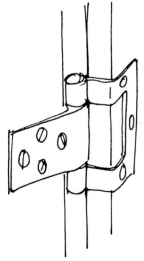

Fig 30 Cranked hinge

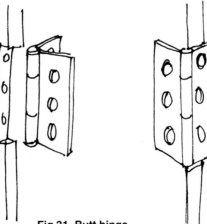

Fig 31 Butt hinge

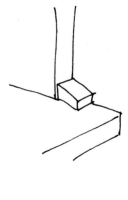

Fig 32 Wedge to support Front

Painting the exterior

The exterior should have been primed before assembly with quick-drying acrylic primer (see page 14). Make sure all the pins are punched in, holes are filled and sanded, and any raw edges are smoothed down. Paint with two coats of vinyl silk emulsion. You will achieve a smoother finish if you paint the Front before the door and windows are fitted, as you can brush straight across. A fine-grained paint roller gives a very smooth finish. Roll the paint again just before it dries to break the bubbles and avoid an 'orange-peel' texture.

Water-based vinyl paint is recommended, as it dries quickly and can be mixed with artist's acrylic colour in small quantities for doors, chimneys, roofs and pavements. Modelmaker's enamel can also be used for the front door.

Before painting the pavement, cover the edge of the varnished floor of the Base with masking tape. If you have used acrylic varnish, the vinyl will take over it, otherwise any excess will have to be sanded off before painting.

Use tinted primer for the exterior of the BRICK and FLINT HOUSES (see pages 36 and 44).

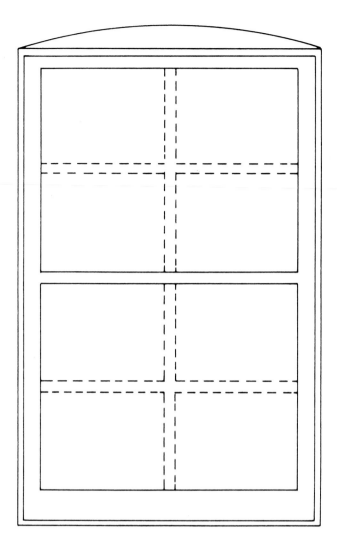

Fig 33 Window plan for BASIC, BRICK and FLINT houses

THE BASIC HOUSE

Having followed the general instructions, you can now complete the BASIC HOUSE. The simple Victorian sash windows and the doorway have stone or brick lintels. The wooden frames are set back to avoid damage by weather, or fire.

Paint the exterior as already recommended, using silk-finish vinyl emulsion.

Walls – choose an attractive colour, not too dark.

Roof – a dark grey; you may need to add more black to a standard colour. Alternatively, mix your own colour.

Roof under the eaves – white.

Pavement and doorstep – add the roof colour to white for a paler grey.

Chimney stacks – same colour as the Walls, with a grey top.

Chimney pots – crimson or terracotta.

Windows, window sills and lintels – paint white before fitting.

Front door – a dark or bright colour. A small tin of modelmaker's enamel is useful.

Windows

These are built up from stripwood, retained inside by an overlapping frame (Fig 34). Clear plastic/perspex sheet and glazing bars fit within the window space, kept in place by more strips glued in the opening (Fig 35).

The bottom bar of each window is ⅛ in x ⅜ in (3 mm x 9 mm), the sides and top ⅛ in x 3/16 in (3 mm x 5 mm) and the glazing bar(s) ⅛ in (3 mm) square. The retaining strips behind are ⅜ in x ⅛ in (9 mm x 3 mm), and ⅛ in x 3/16 in (3 mm x 5 mm) for the interior sill. The optional retainers in front are 1/16 in (1.5 mm) square, the window sill is ¼ in (6 mm) square, and the perspex 1/32 in (1 mm).

You can vary the thickness of the wood, depending on availability. Some strip is measured in millimetres, some in inches. An exact equivalent is not always possible.

Paint the stripwood before cutting. Check the size of the window openings and cut the glazing bars to fit. Mark the joints and cut away to half depth (Fig 36). This is much stronger than making a butt join, particularly when making several panes. It is best to indicate a sash window by crossing the verticals. If you wish to be realistic, vary the cuts so that the sides overlap the top and bottom strips. (Remember the WEATHERBOARD verticals must be in front to take the black window frames.)

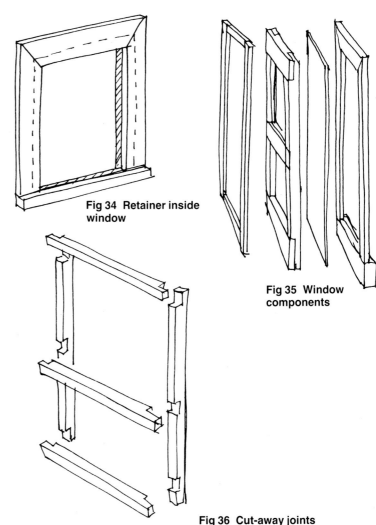

Fig 34 Retainer inside window

Fig 35 Window components

Fig 36 Cut-away joints

Diagram 1 BASIC HOUSE

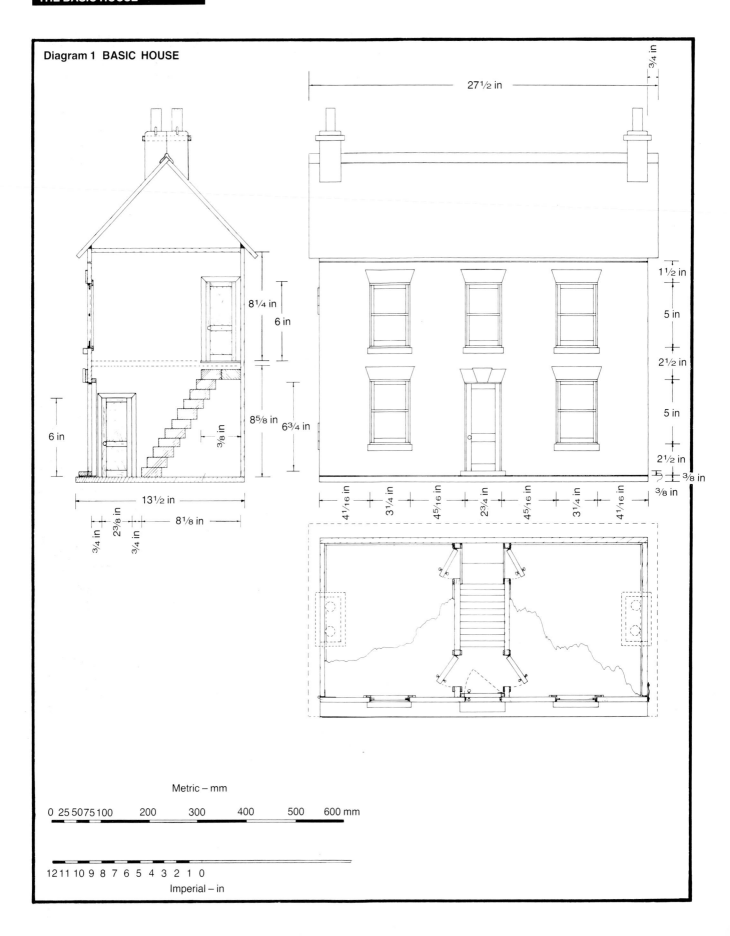

Metric – mm

0 25 50 75 100   200   300   400   500   600 mm

12 11 10 9 8 7 6 5 4 3 2 1 0

Imperial – in

A flat coat of paint finishes the Basic House. This is a sturdy house, suitable for a child to play with, so make sure the paint is non-toxic

Fit retaining wood on the inside, mitring the top corners; this must overlap the hole by ⅛ in (3 mm). Sandwich the perspex between the inside frame and glazing bars, and finish with ¹⁄₁₆ in (1.5 mm) square retainers – two cut full height, two cross-pieces to fit between. The retainer may be left off; it adds realism to a sash window, but casement (hinged) windows are often flush with the glazing bars.

Front door

This is set behind the Front, unlike the Interior Doors which are flush with the walls.

Cut ⅛ in (3 mm) sheet to the exact size of the door opening (6¾ in x 2¾ in/17.2 cm x 7 cm). Add lengths cut from 1/16 in (1.5 mm) sheet, or ½ in x 1/16 in (12 mm x 1.5 mm) strip (Fig 37). Glue the strips in place, and weight down until dry. Repeat on the other side.

Fit the doorknob, then hinge the door to ¼ in (6 mm) square upright, the same height as the door opening. Glue the upright to one side of the opening. Finish the door surround with the other upright and cross-piece (Fig 38). Line the top and sides of the doorway with 1/16 in x 3/16 in (1.5 mm x 5 mm), to stop the door opening outwards against the hinge (Fig 39).

Finish the Front by gluing the doorstep, lintels and window sills in position. The doorstep may need to be rubbed down on the side to be glued, as well as the space below the front door, to make a firm joint. Cut from 3/8 in (9 mm) square, the step is 3½ in (8.9 cm) long on the BASIC and FLINT HOUSES. The BRICK and WEATHERBOARD HOUSES need a 4 in (10 cm) long step to fit the door surround, and the TUDOR HOUSE step is approximately 3¾ in (9.5 cm) long.

The BASIC HOUSE lintels are cut from 1/16 in (1.5 mm) sheet, 1 in (2.5 cm) high and 4 in (10.2 cm) wide at the top, reducing to 3¼ in (8.3 cm) at the bottom. For the centre window and door they are 3½ in (8.9 cm) reducing to 2¾ in (7 cm). The keystone over the Front Door is 1 in (2.5 cm), reducing to 9/16 in (1.4 cm) (Fig 40).

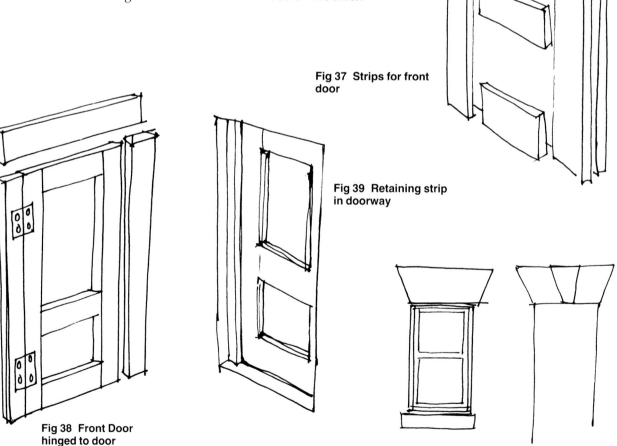

Fig 37 Strips for front door

Fig 39 Retaining strip in doorway

Fig 38 Front Door hinged to door surround

Fig 40 Lintels and keystone

Block stairs

This is the simplest type of staircase, using blocks 1¾ in deep x ¾ in high (44 mm x 19 mm), stepped back ½ in (12 mm) or ¾ in (19 mm), depending on the depth of your house. The floor-to-floor height should be worked out in multiples of ¾ in (19 mm). To fit the BASIC and TUDOR HOUSES, the treads are ½ in (12 mm) deep.

Cut 11 steps 3½ in (8.9 cm) long, plus one more to form the landing if trimmed to a depth of 1⅜ in (3.5 cm); otherwise cut ply to fit. Use a mitre block with a scrap of wood lightly nailed in (or taped if metal or plastic) for a stop, to ensure uniform length (Fig 41). Sand the cut edges, and pencil in a line ½ in (12 mm) from the front edge, as a guide when gluing. Stain and varnish treads and risers, as any surplus glue will seal the wood against the stain. Alternatively, paint them white when assembled, remembering to leave the sides unpainted for gluing.

Glue two steps together. Lay on a flat surface, and tape the first step at an angle against scrap wood. Then glue the other ten steps, applying firm pressure to each joint. Check the angle remains correct, and use a ruler or straight edge to make sure the sides are straight (Fig 42). When dry, join the final block, 1⅜ in (3.5 cm) deep, to form the landing (Fig 43).

These stairs should be built before the final fitting of the Interior Walls and cutting of the Floors (see page 16).

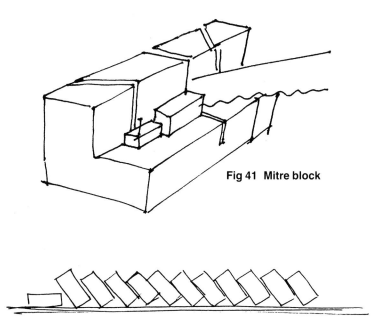

Fig 41 Mitre block

Fig 42 Angled blocks

Fig 43 Block stairs and landing

Interior doors

These are made of ⅛ in (3 mm) sheet, built up with 1/16 in x ½ in (1.5 mm x 12 mm) stripwood, leaving the centre panels recessed as for the front door. Cut to 5⅞ in x 2¼ in (15 cm x 5.7 cm) to fit the block stairs, but cut 6⅜ in (16.2 cm) high for the return stairs. The TUDOR HOUSE has plainer doors.

When the glue is dry, sand and paint or varnish. To avoid the problem of screwing hinges into a narrow doorway, the doors are hung on ⅜ in (9 mm) square strip, which is then glued into place to act as a door jamb. The jamb must fit the opening; the door has a clearance of 1/16 in (1.5 mm) all round.

To fit each hinge, mark the position by folding it round the side of the door. Cut a recess to the depth of the closed hinge with a sharp craft knife (Fig 45). Pilot the screw holes to avoid splitting the wood.

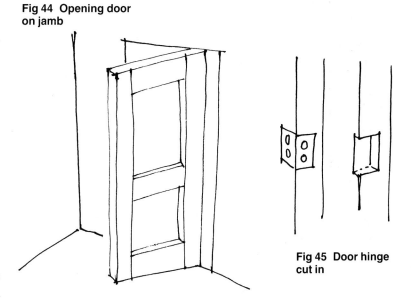

Fig 44 Opening door on jamb

Fig 45 Door hinge cut in

The narrow block stairs are easy to build and allow for larger rooms

Drill small holes for doorknobs, and fix with instant glue. You may need to clip off part of the back pin on one, using the cutting side of pliers, otherwise make sure the knobs are not quite level on each side. More expensive knobs are also available, two threaded on a shank which goes through the door.

Screw the hinge to the door and jamb, remembering to hinge two to the left and two to the right (Fig 46). Doors usually swing into a room, not against the wall, as the doorknob would damage the paint. (Ready-made door kits do not usually allow for this, but can be adapted.) However, at the top of the block stairs, the doors will swing against the wall because the door jambs are set at the back for easier cutting.

Glue the jamb and wedge tightly into position with a small strip of wood braced against the other side of the doorway (Fig 47).

Mitre the architrave at 45°, painting one side and the edges of the stripwood first. This can be ⅛ in x ⅜ in (3 mm x 9 mm) strip scored, or the specially made doll's house moulding. Fit round the doorway inside and out (Fig 48).

The doors upstairs are one step up from the landing, so a $\frac{1}{8}$ in (3 mm) square edging is needed, level with the doorway and cut to the full width of the door surround (Fig 49).

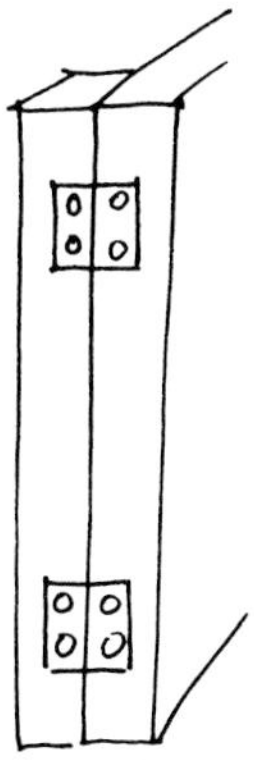

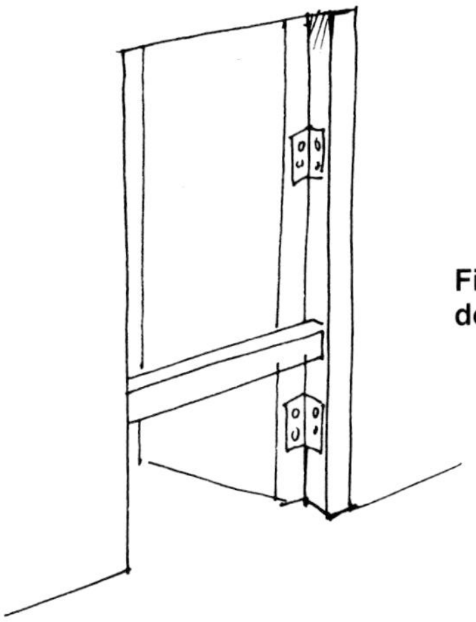

Fig 47 Jamb wedged in doorway

Fig 46 Doors hinged to jambs

Fireplaces

Simple fireplaces can be made of $\frac{1}{8}$ in x $\frac{1}{2}$ in (3 mm x 12 mm) strip, with brackets supporting the mantlepiece cut from astragal moulding or carved (Fig 50). Centre the fireplace on the Side or Back wall. (Many antique houses have this focal point on the back wall even when the chimney is on the side.) Mark the opening and paste black paper in the space, or paint it black before gluing the fireplace in position.

Take care in the block stairs hallway to leave $\frac{3}{8}$ in (9 mm) clearance from the Front, to allow for the front door frame (Fig 51). Skirting, $\frac{1}{8}$ in x $\frac{1}{2}$ in (3mm x 12 mm) strip can be cut square into corners or mitred (Fig 52).

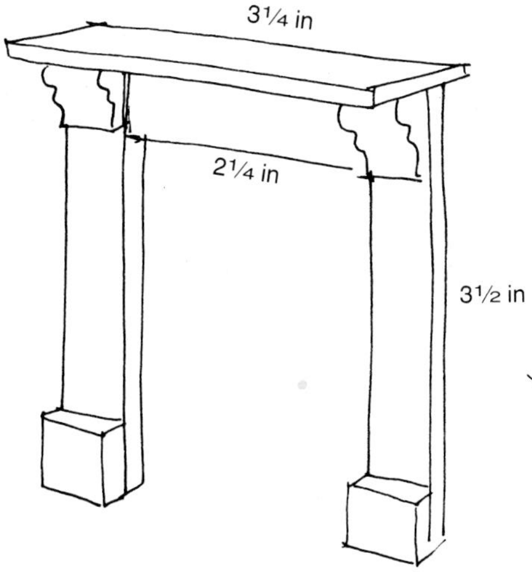

Fig 48 Mitred architrave

Fig 49 Lip for doorway

3$\frac{1}{4}$ in
2$\frac{1}{4}$ in
3$\frac{1}{2}$ in
Fig 50 Fireplace

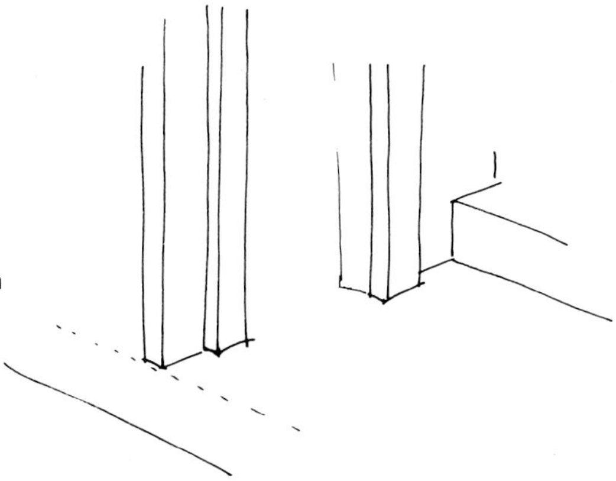

Fig 51 $\frac{3}{4}$ in gap

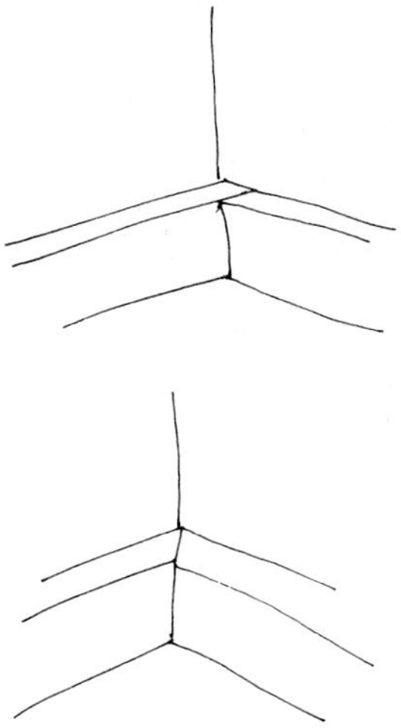

Fig 52 Skirting, mitre or butt

Decorating

The walls should be painted before fitting pre-painted mouldings. Floors should have been varnished before assembly to protect them from paint.

When planning your colour scheme, remember that *all* the rooms will be visible at once and therefore need to co-ordinate. Do not have colours that clash or jar next to each other. Patterns of wallpaper should also balance; this matters more in the SIX-ROOM HOUSE, where you do not want all plain colours one side and all patterns the other (see page 87).

The kitchen is traditionally on the left, which is logical if you look from left to right; you see the food being prepared and then continue to the dining or living room.

Decide on the use of each room before decorating. The kitchen may double as a dining area. Paint it white, or blue which was once considered a deterrent to flies; many antique doll's houses were papered with the blue paper used to pack sugar. It may be best to choose some of your upholstered furniture and bedcovers before deciding on the final colour scheme.

The top floor can have the master bedroom, and either a bathroom or nursery. Most children insist on a bathroom, but do not object to the baby sharing it!

Wallpaper should be cut to the size of the walls. Make sure the pattern fits at the joins, and allow for trimming afterwards around doors and fireplaces (Fig 53). Mix thick wallpaper paste, and brush it on to both

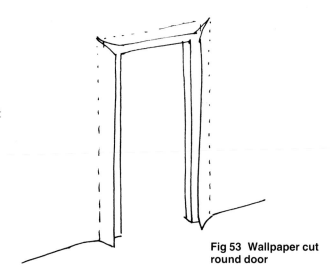

Fig 53 Wallpaper cut round door

paper and walls. If the walls have not been primed, several layers of paste will be needed to seal them, otherwise the paste soaks in, and the paper will not stick. Leave a few minutes for the paper to stretch. Apply a second coat if too dry. Press the wallpaper in place, smoothing out from the centre with a soft cloth. Use a short piece of card or a straight-edged kitchen spatula (wood or plastic) to press out air bubbles and excess paste. When dry, the paper is quite hard and can be trimmed with a craft knife.

If you want to wallpaper inside the Front, measure very carefully to fit each room. You can leave a white strip separating the panels, to coincide with the walls and floor, or butt up.

Your doll's house is now ready for habitation!

THE BRICK HOUSE

There is a strong tradition of building brick houses in England. This was encouraged after the Great Fire of London in 1666, when the wooden and thatch houses burnt like tinder, and a decree was made enforcing the brick cladding of buildings. Previously only the great houses had been built of brick. Suitable clay was available; that, mixed with sand, was cast in wooden moulds, and fired to make it weatherproof.

Many seventeenth-century houses were 'modernized' with Georgian façades. Gainsborough's birthplace in Sudbury, Suffolk, was refaced at some time in the 1700s. It is easy to see where this was done – the top floor windows, suitably positioned under an overhanging roof, now have too high an expanse of brick between them and the top of the parapet extended above them.

With mass production in the nineteenth century, bricks were readily available, and rows of houses were built for the workers who moved to the towns.

The BRICK HOUSE is typically Victorian, with its slate roof and dormer windows. The front windows are all the same size, as the return staircase allows a wider hall. They have four panes, instead of two as in the BASIC HOUSE.

Return Staircase

This consists of two short flights of triangle strip mounted on thin sheet (Fig 54), with a half-landing cut from scrap ply 5³⁄₈ in x 2¹⁄₂ in (13.6 cm x 6.5 cm). The stairwell is cut 6¹⁄₈ in wide x 6¹⁄₄ in deep (15.6 cm x 15.9 cm); the sides are lined by the Interior Walls, which then slot over the front landing.

Stain and varnish the 'tread' and 'riser' of the triangle before cutting. Cut ten lengths 2¹⁄₂ in (6.4 cm) of ³⁄₄ in (1.9 cm) triangle, plus two of ³⁄₈ in (9 mm), using a stop on the mitre block to ensure all are the same length. If no skirting is wanted along the wall, cut the steps to 2⁵⁄₈ in (6.8 cm).

Glue the steps on two panels of ¹⁄₁₆ in (1.5 mm) sheet of ply 5⁷⁄₈ in x 2¹⁄₂ in (15 cm x 6.4 cm), finishing with ³⁄₈ in (9 mm) triangle

where the stair joins the landing. Cut two inner strings, or skirting, ¹⁄₈ in thick x ⁷⁄₈ in (3 mm x 22 mm) and approximately 7¹⁄₂ in (19 cm) long, and two outer strings 5¹⁄₂ in (14 cm) and 6 in (15.2 cm) to fit between the newel posts and support the banisters. Cut as indicated (Fig 55).

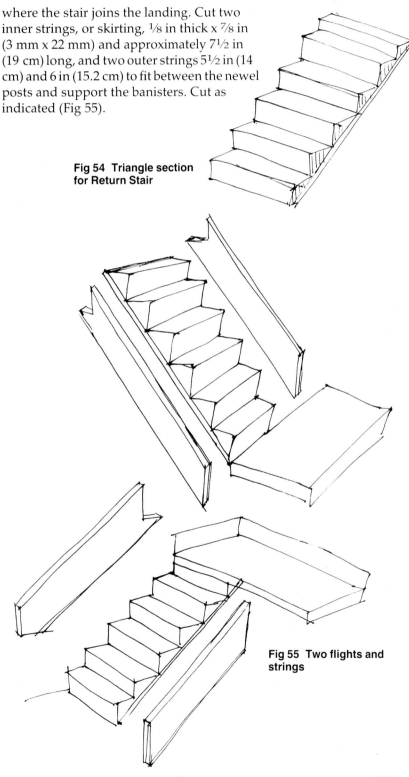

Fig 54 Triangle section for Return Stair

Fig 55 Two flights and strings

Diagram 2 BRICK HOUSE

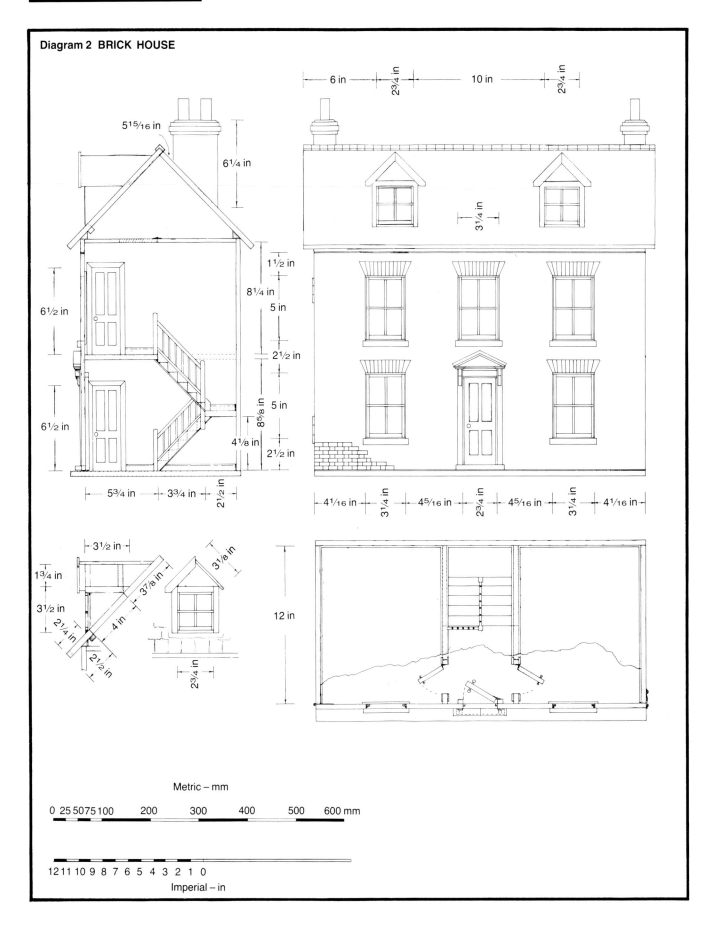

Metric – mm

0 25 50 75 100   200   300   400   500   600 mm

12 11 10 9 8 7 6 5 4 3 2 1 0

Imperial – in

Position the landing 4⅛ in (10.5 cm) up the Back Wall, using spacers and masking tape. Glue the inner string, or skirting, to the side of each flight, and tape the outer strings, which will be needed for assembling the banisters. Check that the stairs fit; some slight adjustment can be made by removing or adding to the skirting of the top flight, which is less visible. Mark the positions for gluing, and decorate or paper round them. (Gluing to primer makes a stronger joint.) Cut and fit ⅛ in (3 mm) x ½ in (12 mm) skirting along the sides and back of the landing, level with the top of the strings. Now make the banisters.

Banisters
If you buy the handrail in a specialist shop, make sure it is already grooved to take the banisters. Alternatively, make up your own, using ½ in (12 mm) half-round hardwood and 1/16 in (1.5 mm) square strip. Glue together as shown (Fig 56), using ⅛ in (3 mm) strip as spacer, the same thickness as the banister. Hold in place with masking tape until dry. Approximately 6 in (15.2 cm) is needed for each flight, plus 2¾ in (7 cm) for the top landing. Sand off the edges with medium, and then fine, sandpaper. Finish with coloured varnish.

Dormer windows and a lift-off roof give extra space in the attic

Fig 56 Handrail

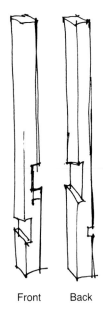

Front   Back

Fig 57 Middle newel

For the newel posts, 12 in (30.5 cm) of ³⁄₈ in (9 mm) square is just enough; cut two lengths 3¼ in (8 cm) for the top and bottom, and 5¼ in (13.3 cm) for the middle. Varnish or paint white. Cut ⅛ in (3 mm) deep notches in the middle newel to fit between the two flights of stairs (Fig 57) starting 3 in (7.6 cm) from the top. Some adjustment may be needed to make them fit (Fig 58). The straight cuts *must* be 1½ in (3.8 cm) apart to fit two steps. The 45° angled cuts may vary to take the extra depth of the backing panels.

The banisters are cut at 45° from ⅛ in (3 mm) square or dowel, using a craft knife. You will need twelve 1¼ in (3.2 cm), plus four cut straight 2¾ in (7 cm) for the top landing. Paint or varnish the strips before cutting, and stand them in Plasticine to dry.

Cut the two handrails and two bottom rails, ³⁄₁₆ in x ¹⁄₁₆ in (5 mm x 1.5 mm), to the same length as the top of the strings, at 45°. Using ruled paper or graph paper as a guide, fit and glue the banisters (Fig 59). Check the angle and hold everything in place with tape or Plasticine while the glue is drying. (Use a quick-setting two-part epoxy resin.)

Check the middle newel for fit with the top and bottom strings. Glue the strings and newel in place. Cut the bottom handrail and banister to fit under the top flight of stairs, using the graph paper as a pattern (Fig 60). Glue the top and bottom banister sets in place, and the bottom newel. When firm, add the top landing banister with the top newel.

If you prefer to use two newels on the half landing, you can peg the banisters into each tread, as in the SIX-ROOM HOUSE, or cut the steps narrower so that both the outer strings butt up to the landing and a newel post.

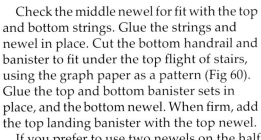

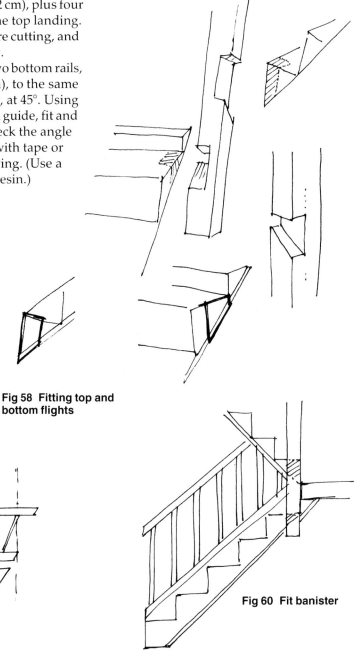

Fig 58 Fitting top and bottom flights

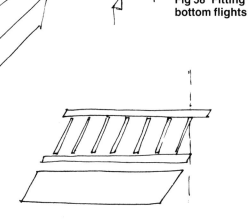

Fig 59 Cut handrail

Fig 60 Fit banister

Lift-off Roof

This is held in position by a batten supported by the ¾ in (19 mm) triangle fixed above the Front Bar (Fig 61). (If you wish to have lower dormers, the Front Roof can be secured with ½ in (12 mm) blocks at each end to correspond with others on the Sides.) Before fixing the Back Roof, mark the position of the batten. Tack a scrap ⅜ in (9 mm) on the back slope of the Sides, and line up the Front Roof (Fig 62). Draw a pencil line where it meets the triangle, then glue and pin the batten in place (Fig 63). You can fix the Back Roof *after* painting the brick. Use the Front Roof instead of scrap for fitting.

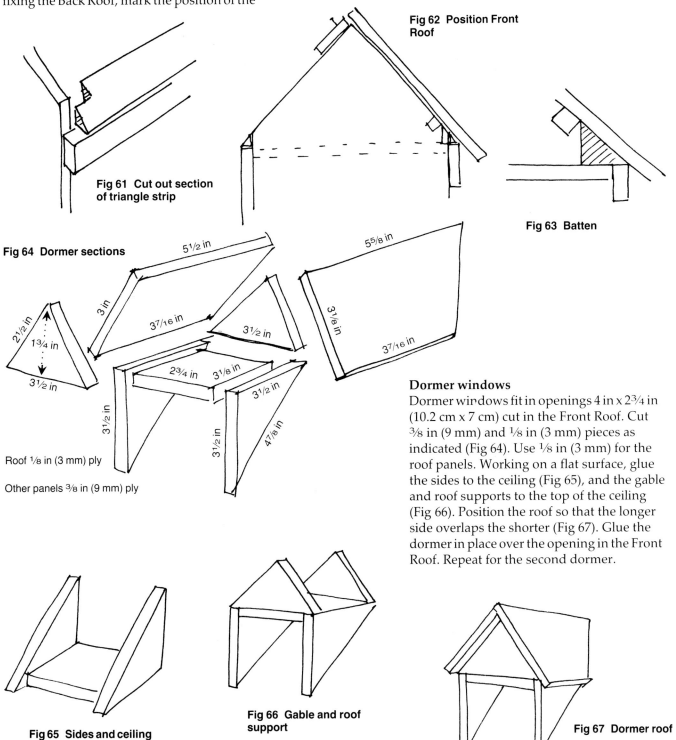

Fig 61 Cut out section of triangle strip

Fig 62 Position Front Roof

Fig 63 Batten

Fig 64 Dormer sections

5½ in

5⅝ in

3 in

2½ in

1¾ in

3½ in

3⁷⁄₁₆ in

3½ in

3⅛ in

3⅛ in

3⁷⁄₁₆ in

2¾ in

3⅛ in

3½ in

3½ in

3½ in

4⅞ in

Roof ⅛ in (3 mm) ply

Other panels ⅜ in (9 mm) ply

Dormer windows

Dormer windows fit in openings 4 in x 2¾ in (10.2 cm x 7 cm) cut in the Front Roof. Cut ⅜ in (9 mm) and ⅛ in (3 mm) pieces as indicated (Fig 64). Use ⅛ in (3 mm) for the roof panels. Working on a flat surface, glue the sides to the ceiling (Fig 65), and the gable and roof supports to the top of the ceiling (Fig 66). Position the roof so that the longer side overlaps the shorter (Fig 67). Glue the dormer in place over the opening in the Front Roof. Repeat for the second dormer.

Fig 65 Sides and ceiling

Fig 66 Gable and roof support

Fig 67 Dormer roof

You can mask the cut edges of the ply with ⅜ in x 1/16 in (9 mm x 1.5 mm) strip around the window. The gable end is covered with ⅜ in x 1/16 in (9 mm x 1.5 mm), 3½ in (8.9 cm) long, mitred and trimmed as indicated (Fig 68). Centre this on the roof panels, to overlap the tiles above and the roof below. Prime the dormers and paint white, except for the roof.

Make the windows from pre-painted ⅛ in square (3 mm) strip and ⅛ in x ⅜ in (3 mm x 9 mm) for the bottom bar. Cut plastic to fit the window opening. Fit from behind, retaining at the top and sides with 1/16 in (1.5 mm) square strip. Add bottom window frames, ⅛ in (3 mm) square, outside, flush with the sides (Fig 69).

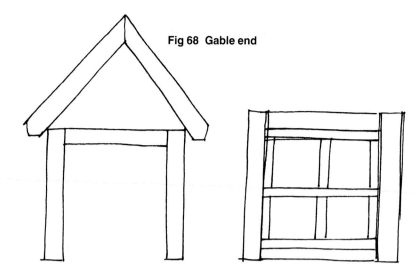

Fig 68 Gable end

Fig 69 Dormer window

Fig 70 Chimney and pots

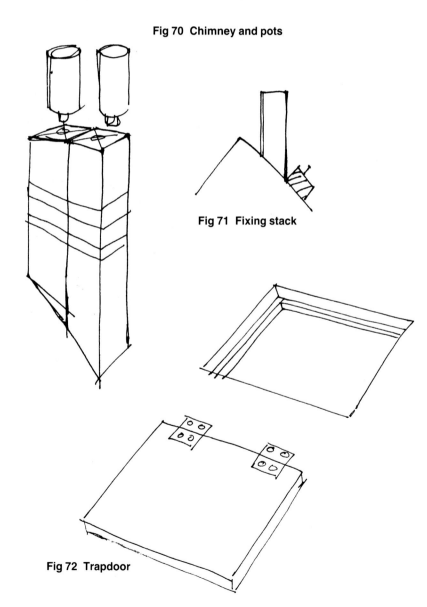

Fig 71 Fixing stack

Fig 72 Trapdoor

Chimneys

These should be fitted before tiling, and stand on the slope of the Back Roof. Once again, cut 2 in x 2 in (5.1 cm x 5.1 cm) at a 45° angle and join to make the stack, but this time the blocks join at the same angle. Cut two lengths of 6¼ in (15.8 cm), and two shorter lengths to fit, to form two stacks. Glue, and tape together until dry (Fig 70). Check the angle is straight against the roof, and sand or plane if necessary. Add 15/16 in (2.4 cm) and 5/16 in (8 mm) strips of ⅛ in (3 mm) just below the bevelled edge of the chimney, to fit three brick courses (see page 18, Fig 27). Paint the brickwork as instructed.

For the chimney pots, see page 18 and Fig 25. For this house, however, they may be turned, or tapered.

To fix the chimneys, line them up with the Sides of the house. Position them 1 in (2.5 cm) from the top of the Back Roof; pin scrap below to stop the stack slipping, then glue in place. Apply pressure with a weight (Fig 71).

Trapdoor in loft

Line the hole with ⅛ in (3 mm) square stop. Cut one piece, 2 7/16 in x 2 15/16 in (6.2 cm x 7.5 cm), or build up in strips and hinge to the floor along the back, (Fig 72).

Bricks

This effect is achieved by painting mottled brick colour over mortar-coloured primer, and then scraping to reveal lines of 'mortar' between the bricks. Acrylic paint and vinyl emulsion must be used throughout. These are water-based, and will not mix with oil-based paints (i.e. those needing white spirit for cleaning).

Paint the assembled house (Sides, Top Bar, Front and chimney stacks) with two coats of ochre-stained acrylic primer. If the inside Front has not yet been primed, paint it with white primer to avoid warping.

When completely dry, apply three thin coats of acrylic artist's colours – burnt sienna (orange-brown), Venetian red (red-brown), raw umber (brown) – stippling with a brush or small sponge. You will need to turn the house to work on each surface, to avoid drip

marks. A hairdryer may speed the drying process.

The bricks are 5/16 in x 7/8 in (8 mm x 22 mm). Scribe in brick 'fans' above each window. Alternatively, protect the panels with masking tape to stop any lines being scribed inadvertently through them, and add the detail last.

As it will be difficult to see any pencil lines on this surface, the measurements can be drawn up on two strips of wood, tacked in place each end of the working surface, and just proud of it. A large T-square is an ideal straightedge, or you could make your own version (Fig 73). Use a small screwdriver or a nail to scrape horizontal lines 5/16 in (8 mm) apart (Fig 74). Repeat vertically, on alternate brick 'courses', every 7/8 in (22 mm). The Front can be removed to work on, but the Sides will need the second batten attached

The lines of mortar are scored, and some bricks painted individually. The door surround is also finely detailed

with masking tape to top and bottom.

Score the bricks above the windows and paint individually. Paint in a few other bricks, for greater realism.

Fit the windows, front door and window sills. The doorstep is 4 in (10 cm) long, to fit the door surround.

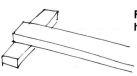

Fig 73 T-square, homemade

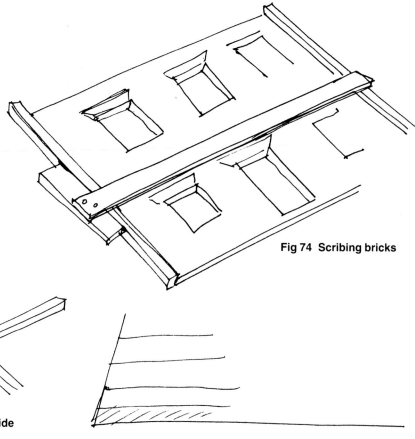

Fig 74 Scribing bricks

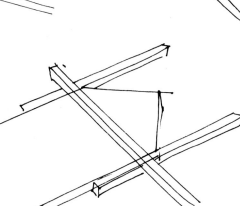

Fig 75 Scribing the Side

Fig 76 Card strip on roof edge

Slates or tiles

Cut ⁷⁄₈ in (22 mm) wide strips of cardboard or ¹⁄₁₆ in (1.5 mm) ply. Every ⁷⁄₈ in (2.2 cm), cut three-quarters across, using scissors or a craft knife on a hard board. Lay these strips along the Roof, starting from the bottom, over-lapping the edge by ¹⁄₈ in (3 mm). Draw the first guideline ³⁄₄ in (19 mm) from the bottom, and the others ⁹⁄₁₆ in (14 mm) apart. Lay a thin strip of card, ¹⁄₄ in (6 mm) wide, along the bottom edge first, to give that row of tiles the same tilt as those overlapping above (Fig 76). Make sure that the tiles and slits alternate in rows, otherwise the roof will leak!

Finish the ridge with birdmouth or plain angle, scored across every ⁷⁄₈ in (2.2 cm) (Fig 77). Tile the dormers, and use card to finish these ridges. Cut a 1 in (2.5 cm) wide strip, fold and snip, and glue over the ridge (Fig 78). The roof should now be painted slate grey. A more realistic effect may be given by picking out some slates in slightly different shades. The roof can also be painted to represent tiles (see the FLINT HOUSE, page 46).

Fig 77 Tiles and ridge

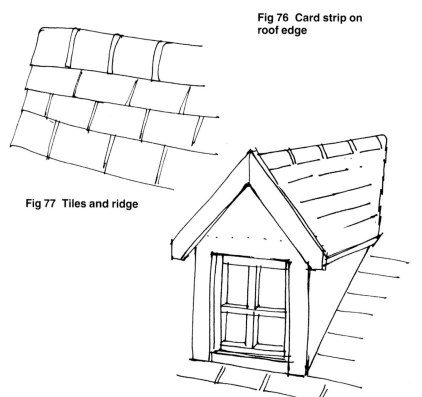

Fig 78 Tiled dormer

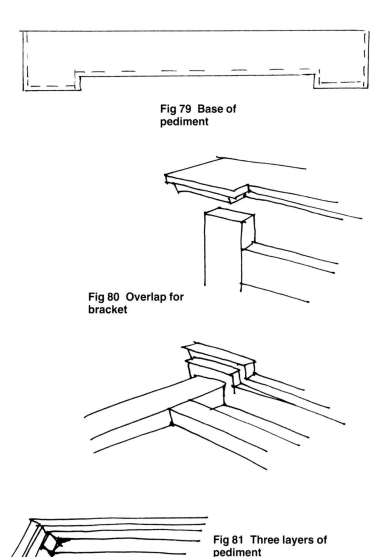

Fig 79 Base of pediment

Fig 80 Overlap for bracket

Fig 81 Three layers of pediment

Fig 82 Bracket and angled top

Porch

The pediment is built up with the lower panel cut slightly smaller to give a moulded edge. The curly brackets are slices of astragal moulding; alternatively, they can be carved out of ⅛ in (3 mm).

The door surround is ¹⁄₁₆ in x ⅜ in (1.5 mm x 9 mm). Cut the sides 7⅜ in (18.7 cm) high. Lay the house on its Back, or the Front flat, and glue the surround in place. The base of the pediment is cut from two strips of ¹⁄₁₆ in (1.5 mm) ply, 4⅛ in and 4 in (10.5 cm and 10.2 cm) wide x ¹¹⁄₁₆ in and ⅝ in (18 mm and 15 mm) deep (Fig 79). The centre, ¾ in (19 mm) from each end, is recessed ⅛ in (3 mm). Glue the smaller panel, which is cut ¹⁄₁₆ in (1.5 mm) shorter all round, below the larger to form a moulded edge. Check that the wider sections fit above the door surround – the support brackets centre on the uprights (Fig 80). They can be made from ⅛ in (3 mm) slices of astragal moulding topped with a strip of ⅛ in (3 mm) square.

The top of the pediment is built of two 2½ in (6.4 cm) lengths of ⅛ in x ⅝ in (3 mm x 15 mm) and ¹⁄₁₆ in x ½ in (1.5 mm x 12 mm), supported at the back by ⅛ in (3 mm) square (Fig 81). It joins the base at an angle of 25°, so the top joint is not a right angle. You will have to draw the vertical and check the wood before cutting the top angle. The top strip is cut square at the bottom, angled at the joint; the other strips are angled top and bottom, and should be easy to cut with a knife before gluing (Fig 82). Cut thin card to fill the triangle and gap between the pediment and the door surround.

THE WEATHERBOARD HOUSE

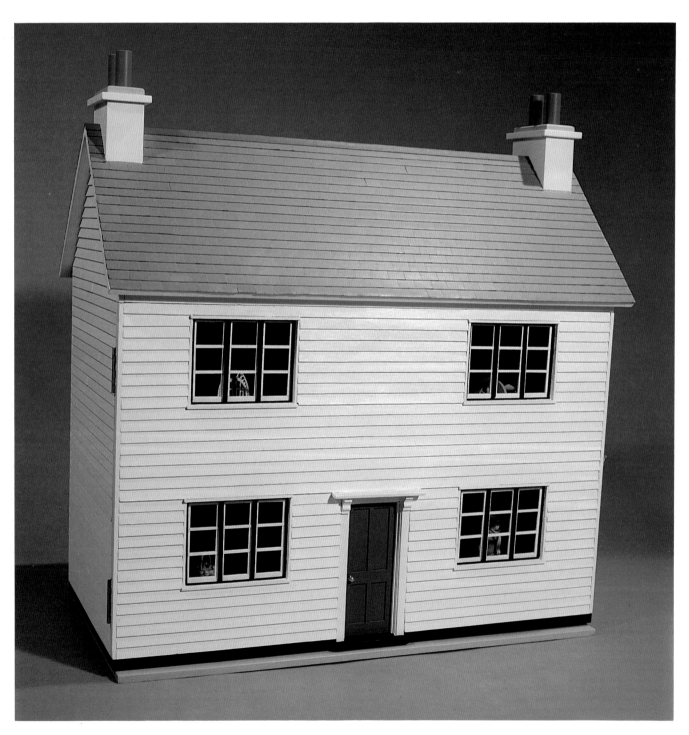

*This simple exterior needs only four casement windows, the
top ones set as close to the roof as possible*

Diagram 3 WEATHERBOARD HOUSE

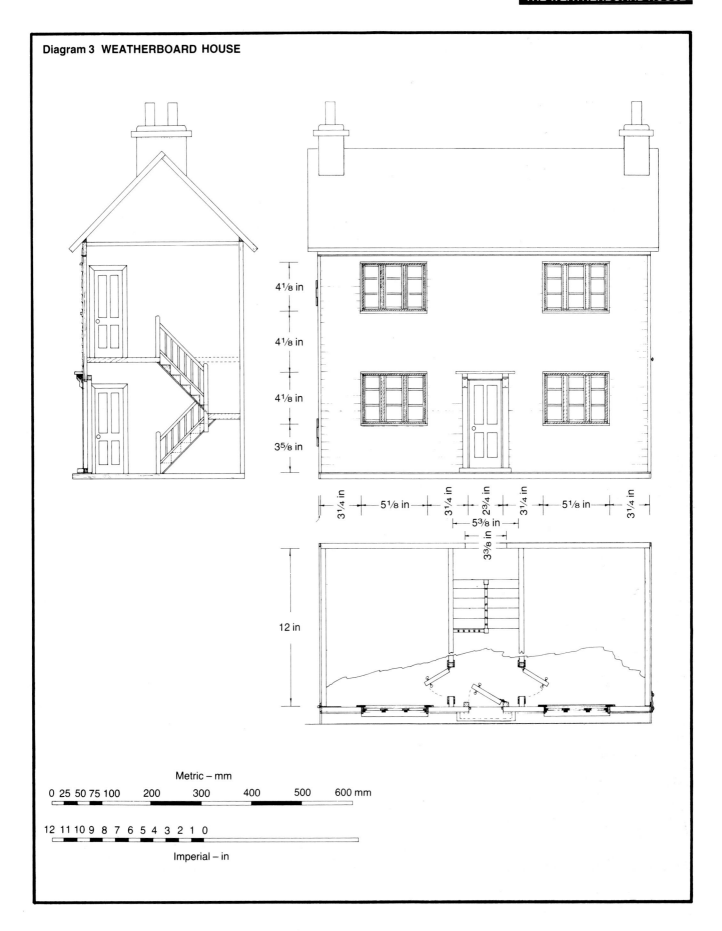

4¹⁄₈ in

4¹⁄₈ in

4¹⁄₈ in

3⁵⁄₈ in

3¹⁄₄ in   5¹⁄₈ in   3¹⁄₄ in   2³⁄₄ in   3¹⁄₄ in   5¹⁄₈ in   3¹⁄₄ in

5³⁄₈ in

3³⁄₈ in

12 in

Metric – mm

0 25 50 75 100   200   300   400   500   600 mm

12 11 10 9 8 7 6 5 4 3 2 1 0

Imperial – in

The overlapping strips of wood protect the walls, and were often added to earlier lath and plaster to keep the weather out. In the days before damp courses, a brick footing was sometimes used for the bottom few feet of the wall, otherwise the bottom board was coated with tar, which was also used for protecting weatherboard barns.

The early settlers in America, finding so much woodland, used wood instead of mud or brick to build their houses, and many 'clapboard' seventeenth-century houses still survive in New England. Weatherboard is also typical of cottages in Kent and Sussex.

The WEATHERBOARD HOUSE has a slate roof that looks Victorian, but earlier tiles are equally suitable. The outside is painted white. As the casement windows are wider than sash ones, the house looks better with only four – to light the stairs, you can cut a window in the Back (see page 13, Fig 3) above the half-landing.

Weatherboard

The weatherboard is ½ in (12 mm) trailing edge balsa (i.e. cut at an angle). You will need fifty 3 ft (91.5 cm) lengths. If you cannot buy this, overlap ½ in x ⅟₁₆ in (12 mm x 1.5 mm), which may mean you cannot keep a straight line above windows and door, or cut a ⅟₁₆ in (1.5 mm) sheet of ply into ⅝ in (16 mm) strips.

Rule guidelines just over ½ in (12 mm) apart – an extra ⅟₁₆ in (1.5 mm) every 2 in (5.1 cm) – to line up with the openings. The tops of the windows and the door canopy should fit below the line of weatherboard.

The corners are protected with hardwood strips. Edge the Front with ⅛ in x ⅜ in (3 mm x 9 mm), faced with ³⁄₁₆ in x ⅛ in (5 mm x 3 mm). Add ⅛ in (3 mm) square to the ends of each Side, to contain the extra depth of the weatherboard (Fig 83).

Cut the window linings from ½ in x ⅛ in (12 mm x 3 mm) – top and bottom to full width (5⅛ in/13 cm), and uprights to fit between (3⅞ in/9.8 cm) – but do not glue until the weatherboard is fitted and can be trimmed along the openings (Fig 84). The top and bottom linings should extend ⅟₁₆ in (1.5 mm) beyond the weatherboard to form rainstrips and window sills. (You can use ⅛ in (3 mm) sheet cut to depth.)

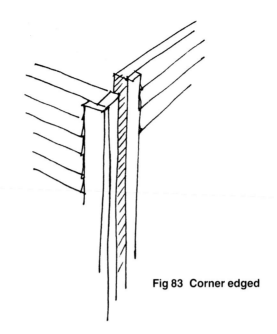

Fig 83 Corner edged

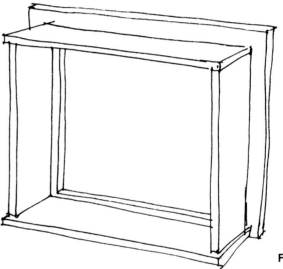

Fig 84 Window lining

Front door

A simple doorway may be lined in the same way, with ⅛ in (3 mm) brackets supporting the canopy (Fig 85).

To make a wider door surround, cut two uprights 7⅛ in (18 cm) high from ⅛ in x ½ in (3 mm x 12 mm) and ½ in (12 mm) wide astragal brackets, supporting a ½ in x ⅛ in (12 mm x 3 mm) canopy, 4¾ in (12 cm) long (3¾ in/9.5 cm for the simple doorway) (Fig 86). Fit the doorway and Front Door as before, but leave the canopy until the weatherboard is cut to fit below (Fig 87).

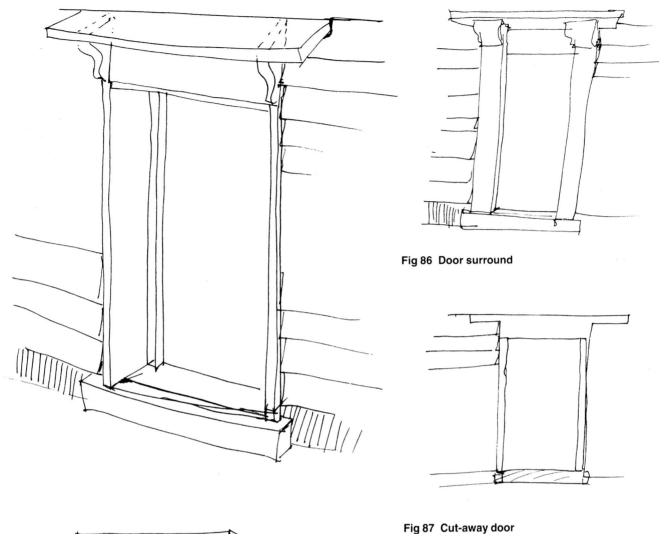

Fig 86 Door surround

Fig 87 Cut-away door canopy

Fig 85 Simple front door

Fitting weatherboard

Start at the bottom with a flat strip of ⅛ in x ½ in (3 mm x 12 mm) (the 'tarred' base protects the wood), then glue the strips of weatherboard in place, using contact adhesive. You should find that six strips of weatherboard (plus the bottom strip) fit below the window, eight to each window, eight between, and one along the top, plus one or one and a half along the Front Bar. Keep any joins in the weatherboard along the Sides.

The doorstep (4 in or 3½ in/10 cm or 8.9 cm, depending on the width of the door surround) should be painted black to match the 'tarred' strip.

The window lining projects top and bottom to deflect the rain

Windows

Now fix the window linings and door canopy. Make up the windows with ³/₁₆ in x ⅛ in (5 mm x 3 mm) for the sides and top, ¼ in x ⅛ in (6 mm x 3 mm) for the bottom, two ⅜ in x ⅛ in (9 mm x 3 mm) uprights, and two cross-pieces of ⅛ in (3 mm) square, pre-painted white. The uprights *must* cross in front of the horizontals to make a flat surface for the black-painted window frames, two ³/₁₆ in x ¹/₁₆ in (5 mm x 1.5 mm) uprights in the centre, ¹/₁₆ in (1.5 mm) square round the sides (Fig 88).

The clear plastic glazing may need to be cut to the whole 4⅛ in (10.5 cm) height x 4⅞ in (12.4 cm) wide to fit the space left by the projecting top and bottom linings. Retain from behind as before, and glue the window frame in front.

Use 2 in (5.1 cm) butt hinges to hang the Front.

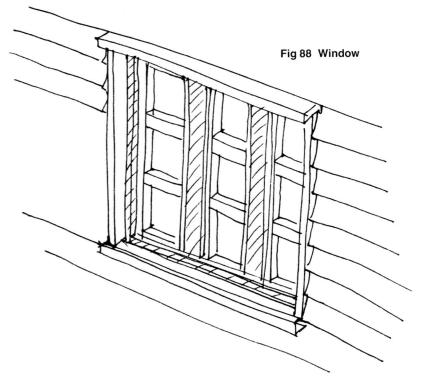

Fig 88 Window

Roof
Use grey-painted card slates, as for the BRICK HOUSE (see page 36), with card ridge tiles.

Chimney
As the BASIC HOUSE (see page 18).

A modern family with a taste for traditional pine furniture. These dolls are German, and the furniture is all handmade by British craftsmen

THE FLINT HOUSE

Flint starts as large pale pebbles, which are split or sliced to give a flat surface. It is very hard-wearing, but being uneven has to be retained by brick corners and edging. It is sometimes set in neat rows or patterns, but this house has random flintwork.

Flint houses are often seen in the south of England and in East Anglia, where the flintstones are frequently turned up in the soil. Many towns and villages still have a fifteenth-century flint church.

Windows
These have 12 panes, a curved brick top, radius 7 in (17.8 cm), and a black frame.

Roof
The roof has decorative ridge tiles. The chimney is 1¼ in (3.2 cm) taller, with three brick courses round the top. There are bargeboards on the gable ends.

Front Door
This house has a tiled porch.

Exterior
The outside is painted to resemble bricks and flint.

Flint
Paint the Sides and Front with two coats of ochre-stained acylic primer, rubbed down (as the BRICK HOUSE background). Draw in brickwork round windows and corners, 5/16 in x 7/8 in (8 mm x 22 mm) wide, with half bricks outlining the windows.

If you wish to texture the walls with a fine spatter effect, cover the bricks with a template kept in place by masking tape held through punched holes (Fig 89), or cover with masking tape. Mix thin solutions of raw umber and Venetian red acrylic paint, and flick from a toothbrush. Test the effect first on scrap paper.

When dry, remove the masking and seal with two coats of matt acrylic varnish. Paint in the brickwork, using thin washes of acrylic burnt sienna, Venetian red and raw umber. When dry, scribe with a fine screwdriver or a nail to reveal the mortar colour (see page 35).

The flint shapes are made by applying partly mixed black, white and ochre acrylic paint with a cranked palette knife. Used straight from the tube, this gives a streaky effect. Any unwanted paint can be wiped or scraped off the varnished surface.

Another method is to mix several greys, and paint pebble shapes on to the base colour. You could use brick paper for the edging, but it must be flat red, not mottled brick. There is a pebble-embossed wallpaper available, but this would need the bricks built out to match.

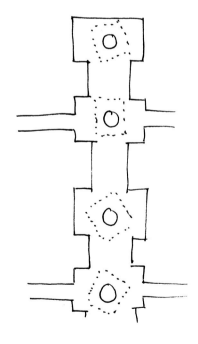

Fig 89 Masking

Diagram 4 FLINT HOUSE

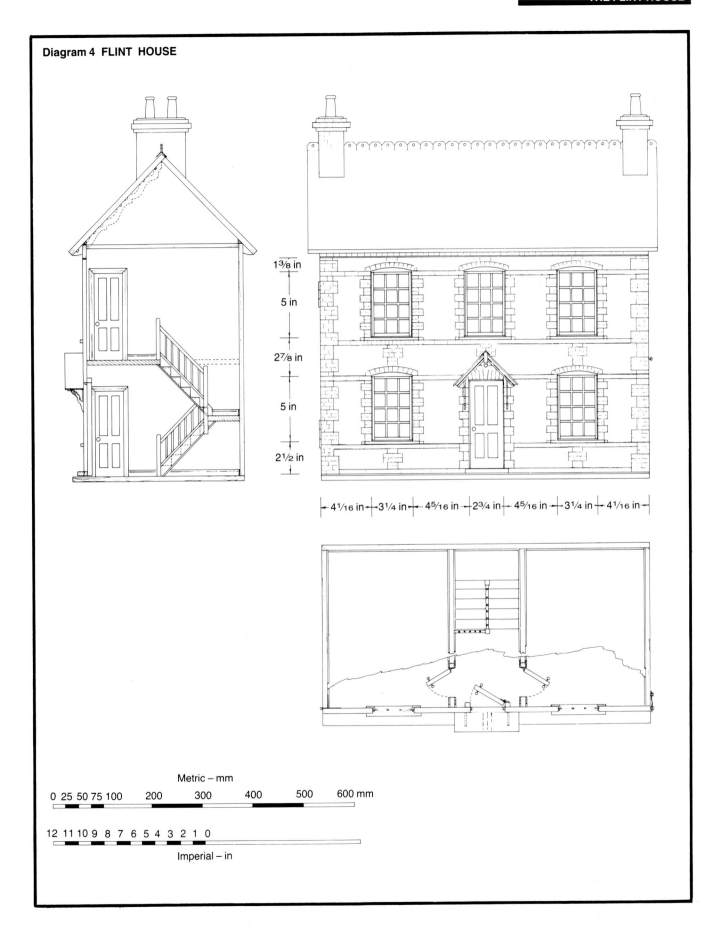

1³⁄₈ in

5 in

2⁷⁄₈ in

5 in

2¹⁄₂ in

4¹⁄₁₆ in — 3¹⁄₄ in — 4⁵⁄₁₆ in — 2³⁄₄ in — 4⁵⁄₁₆ in — 3¹⁄₄ in — 4¹⁄₁₆ in

Metric – mm

0 25 50 75 100   200   300   400   500   600 mm

12 11 10 9 8 7 6 5 4 3 2 1 0

Imperial – in

This house of brick and flint is amazingly realistic, with its decorative ridge tiles and bargeboards, and turned chimney pots

Looking at real houses will give you all sorts of ideas for other textures and finishes – these photographs show London brick, random Cotswold stone, and Essex flint

Porch

Mitre two $3\frac{1}{8}$ in (8 cm) strips of $\frac{1}{8}$ in x $1\frac{3}{8}$ in (3 mm x 35 mm) to meet at right angles – or cut one side 3 in (7.6 cm) and overlap, as the roof. Glue together, using a 1 in (2.5 cm) length of $\frac{1}{4}$ in (6 mm) square to strengthen the joint (Fig 90). Add strips of $\frac{1}{16}$ in (1.5 mm) and $\frac{1}{8}$ in (3 mm) square stepped back $\frac{1}{16}$ in (1.5 mm) from the front edge, to form a moulding (Fig 91). Mitre the joint with a knife. Add a decorative finial cut to fit (Fig 92). Tile the roof, and support it on $\frac{1}{8}$ in (3 mm) brackets (Fig 93), level with the top of the door.

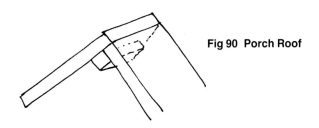

Fig 90 Porch Roof

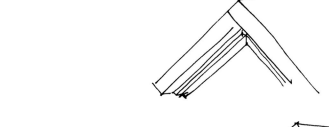

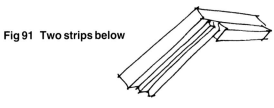

Fig 91 Two strips below

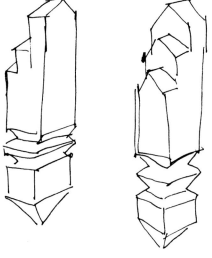

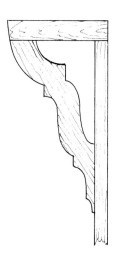

Fig 93 Bracket template

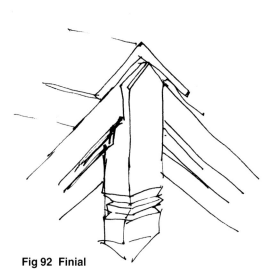

Fig 92 Finial

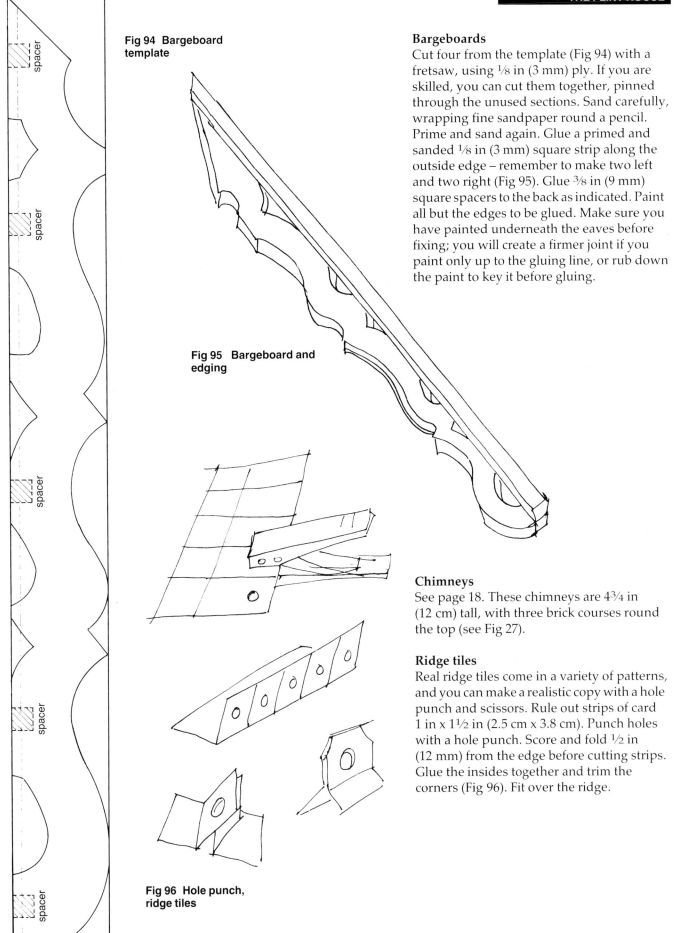

Fig 94 Bargeboard template

Fig 95 Bargeboard and edging

Fig 96 Hole punch, ridge tiles

spacer

Bargeboards

Cut four from the template (Fig 94) with a fretsaw, using ⅛ in (3 mm) ply. If you are skilled, you can cut them together, pinned through the unused sections. Sand carefully, wrapping fine sandpaper round a pencil. Prime and sand again. Glue a primed and sanded ⅛ in (3 mm) square strip along the outside edge – remember to make two left and two right (Fig 95). Glue ⅜ in (9 mm) square spacers to the back as indicated. Paint all but the edges to be glued. Make sure you have painted underneath the eaves before fixing; you will create a firmer joint if you paint only up to the gluing line, or rub down the paint to key it before gluing.

Chimneys

See page 18. These chimneys are 4¾ in (12 cm) tall, with three brick courses round the top (see Fig 27).

Ridge tiles

Real ridge tiles come in a variety of patterns, and you can make a realistic copy with a hole punch and scissors. Rule out strips of card 1 in x 1½ in (2.5 cm x 3.8 cm). Punch holes with a hole punch. Score and fold ½ in (12 mm) from the edge before cutting strips. Glue the insides together and trim the corners (Fig 96). Fit over the ridge.

Bricks are used to edge the windows and strengthen the corners. Decorative bargeboards protect the gable ends

50

As there is no room for a dining room as well as a bathroom in a four-room house, this Victorian house has a jug and bowl in the bedroom and would have a hip bath in the kitchen

THE TUDOR HOUSE

The oak forests used to build the Elizabethan fleet also supplied the timber for houses. Their basic framework was built from great baulks of unseasoned oak, which tended to warp while drying – hence the uneven lines of the timbers. The walls were filled in with wattle and daub – thin staves and mud, straw and dung – protected by a layer of lime plaster. Many of the attractive timbered houses you now see were originally plastered all over to protect the wood, and the studs (uprights) show holes where the laths were nailed across to key the plaster.

This house has a steeper roof than the others. The gable ends are taller and cut down at a sharper angle.

Inglenook fireplace
This should be cut out of the left Side before assembly – 4 in x 4½ in (10.2 cm x 11.5 cm) – and should be ⅝ in (15 mm) above ground level.

Stairs
This house has block stairs.

Doors
These are scored (or made from strip) instead of panelled.

Floors
Draw 1 in (2.5 cm) wide floorboards, and colour with Oak stain or varnish.

Windows
These are leaded by scoring and applying black paint.

Studwork
The studwork on the outside is made of veneer or thin ply stained with dark oak. This can also be used inside.

Roof
Bevel the ridge and thatch the roof with raffia.

Chimney stack
This is built out from the Side Wall (one only). The stack on the ridge is 7 in (17.8 cm) high. Cut 2 in (5.1 cm) square planed softwood (see page 18) but at a sharper angle (Fig 97). Mark the angle on the wood by checking it against the roof slope. Glue the two sections together (Fig 98). Cut the ridge back to the Side Wall, to the width of the chimney (Fig 99); a sharp chisel may be needed to trim it vertical.

A ⅜ in (9 mm) batten is added to the side of the chimney and Side Wall to make the outline of the brick chimney. First cut the ⅜ in (9 mm) chimney panel and trace round for an exact match (Fig 100). If you need a fireplace deeper than ¾ in (19 mm) to fit a firebasket or firedogs, increase the depth of the batten.

Tudor bricks are shallower than usual ones; ¼ in (6 mm) courses give 3 in (7.6 cm) in scale. Build up strips of 1/16 in (1.5 mm) and ⅛ in (3 mm) round the top, extending it ¼ in (6 mm) above to leave a recess; glue and hold with tape (Fig 101). Paint and score the bricks (see page 35).

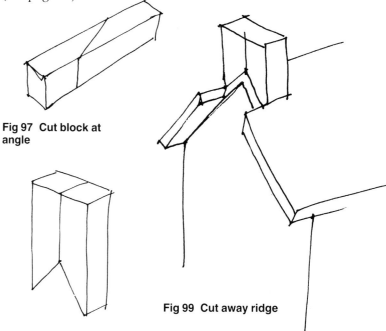

Fig 97 Cut block at angle

Fig 99 Cut away ridge

Fig 98 Joined for stack

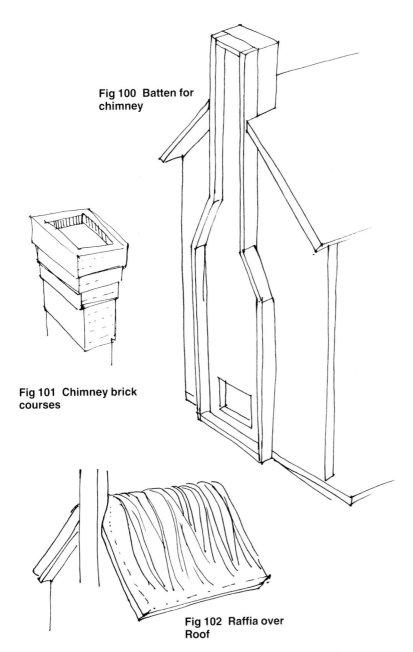

Fig 100 Batten for chimney

Fig 101 Chimney brick courses

Fig 102 Raffia over Roof

Thatch

Real thatch can be between 1-2ft (30-60 cm) thick. Build up the roof with two panels of 1¼ in (3.2 cm) strawboard or layers of corrugated paper, finishing smooth side out. Sculpt round the side of the chimney. Paste the roof with wood glue, then lay strands of raffia down the roof (Fig 102). The outer slope should overhang, level with the inner edge, for the rain to run off.

For the ridge trim, cut scrap fabric to a scalloped shape. Lay 10 in (25 cm) lengths of raffia across and, using a large darning or upholstery needle, start with a back stitch to hold, and continue in cross stitch for decoration (Fig 103). Trim the raffia to shape. Fit over the ridge between the chimney and the gable end (Fig 104). Tuck the raffia round and down the side of the chimney, and round off the edges of the gables. Trim horizontally along the front and back of the overhang.

If you want to 'weather' the thatch, the raffia can be coloured with diluted spirit-based woodstain before thatching. Test a small amount first.

I have also seen a coconut matting doormat used convincingly as thatch; you would have to leave off the ridge trim. Long-pile carpet stiffened with glue and painted is effective (but not fur fabric), or you could even use long-pile towelling, built up over the corrugated paper (corrugations upward) and painted. Plaster can be used, scored and textured to simulate thatch.

Tiles would also be suitable for this house.

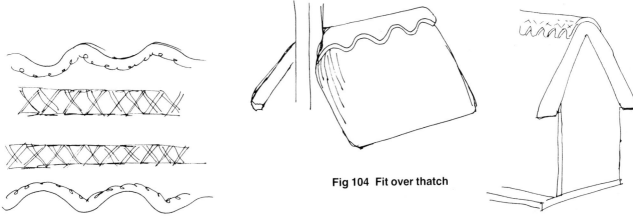

Fig 103 Ridge pattern

Fig 104 Fit over thatch

A thatched roof needs a steeper slope for the rain to run off

The studwork must be uneven to appear centuries old

Outside Walls

These are usually white, sometimes colour-washed pink or a cream – use silk vinyl emulsion as usual. For the timbers, stain $\frac{1}{16}$ in and $\frac{3}{64}$ in (1.5 mm and 1 mm) sheet or veneer with Jacobean Dark Oak stain and seal with matt varnish. Cut strips approximately $\frac{5}{8}$ in and $\frac{1}{2}$ in (15 mm and 12 mm) wide. Try out the position of the timbers before gluing. Use the diagram as reference.

Windows

Cut plastic to fit. Score a diamond pattern with a very small sharp screwdriver or nail. Paint black and wipe off any surplus carefully before the paint is totally dry. The window frame is $\frac{1}{8}$ in x $\frac{3}{16}$ in (3 mm x 5 mm), the bottom rail $\frac{1}{8}$ in x $\frac{3}{8}$ in (3 mm x 9 mm) and the central glazing bars $\frac{1}{8}$ in (3 mm) square.

Diagram 5 TUDOR HOUSE

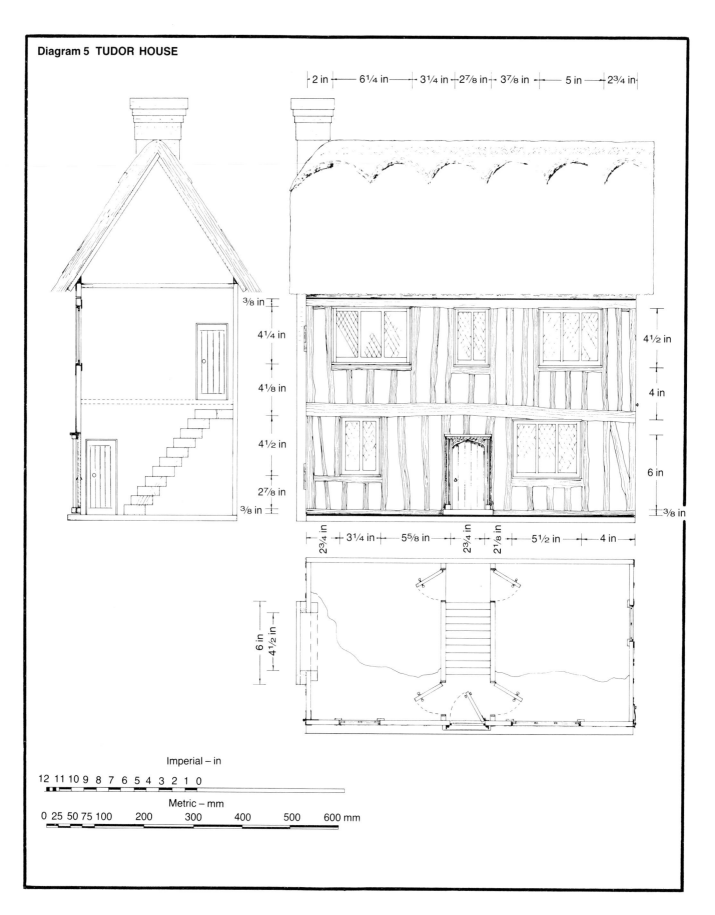

Imperial – in

12 11 10 9 8 7 6 5 4 3 2 1 0

Metric – mm

0 25 50 75 100   200   300   400   500   600 mm

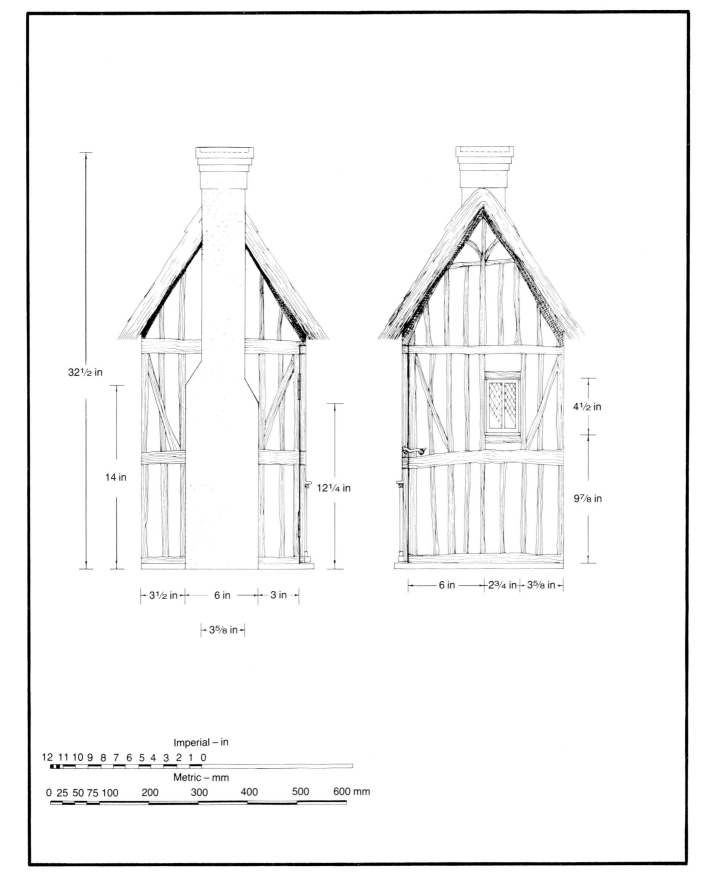

32½ in

14 in

12¼ in

⊢ 3½ in ⊣ 6 in ⊢ 3 in ⊣

⊢ 3⅝ in ⊣

4½ in

9⅞ in

⊢ 6 in ⊢ 2¾ in ⊢ 3⅝ in ⊣

Imperial – in

12 11 10 9 8 7 6 5 4 3 2 1 0

Metric – mm

0 25 50 75 100   200   300   400   500   600 mm

Front Door

Cut two $5^{15}/_{16}$ in x $2^{11}/_{16}$ in (15.1 cm x 6.8 cm) of $1/_8$ in (3 mm) sheet to fit within the doorway. Score vertically to simulate planks, and glue back to back.

The doorframe may be simple uprights and a cross-piece, but a little period detail can be added to give more interest (Fig 105).

For the moulding above the door, tape together two thicknesses of mahogany (you need a hardwood to carve this detail) $1/_{32}$ in and $1/_8$ in (1 mm and 3 mm), cut to $2^3/_4$ in x $7/_8$ in (7 cm x 2.2 cm). Cut away the inside curve with a knife or fretsaw, and remove the tape. Cut carefully round the top of $1/_{32}$ in (1 mm) panel, making short downward strokes with a very sharp knife, leaving $1/_{16}$ in (1.5 mm) 'moulding' to fit on the front of the $1/_8$ in (3 mm) panel. Finish with $1/_{32}$ in x $1/_{16}$ in (1 mm x 1.5 mm) strip along the top edge (Fig 106).

Set the panel in the top of the doorway, flush with the sides. The carved woodwork round the door is built up with shaped or carved strips. Tudor joints were not mitred. The uprights are made of small astragal with one side cut off, plus $1/_8$ in (3 mm) square strip; the top strips are $1/_8$ in x $1/_4$ in (3 mm x 6 mm) and $1/_8$ in (3 mm) square. A carved pattern can be made with a nail, for a round indentation, or a screwdriver or knife for a V-cut. Other decoration can be made with dark 'plastic wood', moulded with a pointed tool or cocktail stick. Paint to match the oak-stained woodwork. Finish with matt varnish. Hang the front door from behind as usual, with the hinges flat on the door and the inside Front.

Internal Doors

These are also scored on both sides, and may be cross-banded with $1/_4$ in x $1/_{16}$ in (6 mm x 1.5 mm) strip on the stair side or may simply have a plank top and bottom (Fig 107).

Inglenook fireplace

This is built up with brick pillars supporting the large oak beam, and one course of bricks forming the hearth (Fig 108).

For the pillars, cut two scraps of $3/_8$ in (9 mm), 4 in high x $3/_4$ in wide (10.2 cm x 19 mm). For the hearth, cut $1/_4$ in (6 mm) sheet to $4^1/_2$ in x $1^1/_8$ in (11.5 cm x 2.9 cm). Paint bricks on one face and the edges. Cut three panels of $1/_{16}$ in (1.5 mm) ply or card to

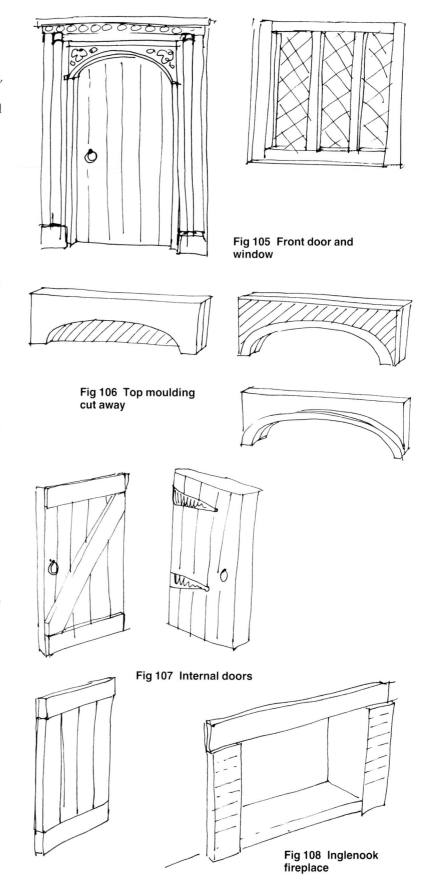

Fig 105 Front door and window

Fig 106 Top moulding cut away

Fig 107 Internal doors

Fig 108 Inglenook fireplace

fit the back and sides of the recess. Paint and match the scribing with the bricks on the side pillars; the back panel may be almost black. Cut the 6 in (15.2 cm) oak beam out of ¼ in x ⅝ in (6 mm x 15 mm), and stain. If you want to use the beam as a mantlepiece, add another layer of ⅛ in or ³⁄₁₆ in (3 mm or 4.5 mm). A few twigs make very good logs.

Interior Walls

These are usually white, but may be painted in pink or a pale yellow. You can add ⅛ in x ½ in (3 mm x 12 mm) beams to the ceiling. First rub down the corners and take a few slices off the sides. The beams must go *across* the line of the floorboards above, as they are supposed to be supporting them. For the studwork (uprights) on the walls, use the ³⁄₆₄ in (1 mm) sheet of veneer that was used on the exterior.

Use the block stairs in this house. A side window gives extra light. The seventeenth-century oak furniture and hand-thrown pottery make this a real period piece, but you could furnish it in any style

THE SIX-ROOM HOUSE

This house has larger rooms, 12¼ in x 15¾ in (31 cm x 40 cm), and is a town house rather than a country cottage. The overall size is 43¾ in high x 34 in wide x 20 in deep (110.5 cm x 86.3 cm x 50.8 cm).

You could adapt the BASIC or BRICK designs by adding one more floor, using the return staircase. However, this house has a more elegant staircase, 7 in (17.8 cm) wide. All the rooms have chimney breasts to allow for recessed fireplaces.

The Roof is set back between the Side walls, as in a terraced house. There is quoining down the sides, and the ground floor has rusticated (grooved) stucco (not pebbledash!) and a portico over the front door.

The upper floors are yellow brick but they could also be plain stucco (smooth rendering), either painted a light colour or the same cream as the 'stonework'. Many London houses are finished in this way to protect the brick.

The house is typical of the Georgian style popular around 1840. A detached Georgian house would have bevelled stone slabs, fanning out above the ground floor windows, which were usually arched at the top. The upper floors and chimneys would be red brick, and the quoins would continue round the corners. The top balustrade could have 'stone' balusters round a flat roof. (The actual shallow roof is seldom visible from below.)

The weight of this house, approximately 70 lb (32 kg), is too much to be supported by a single sheet of ⅜ in (9 mm) ply, so it is mounted on a base of 2 in x 1½ in (5.1 cm x 3.8 cm) softwood. This makes lifting it much easier as there is an edge to grip underneath.

Preparation

Cut panels as shown (Fig 110). Allow at least ¹⁄₁₆ in (1.5 cm) between the drawn lines for the sawcut. The Back panel can be the same height as the Front, but the Back Roof is easier to tile if the Back is level with the Top. If you can mitre the ridge at 60°, cut the Roof panels

about ⅜ in (9 mm) deeper. This also applies if you use thinner plywood: ⅛ in (3 mm) can be used for the Roof. The landings will be cut to size when the staircase is constructed.

Cut the internal door openings to fit available kits (Fig 109). The ones used were 6¹⁵⁄₁₆ in x 2¹⁵⁄₁₆ in (17.7 cm x 7.5 cm), or you can make your own (see page 25). This size allows for a ⅛ in (3 mm) threshold and lining to the doorway. If you do not want the dolls to trip over this step(!), remove the strip below the door and cut down the door surround. You can cover the cut edge of the ply with veneer, thin ply or stripwood: recess this into the floor by cutting the door opening to that extra depth.

Fig 109 Door kit

8 ft x 4 ft ³⁄₈ in birch ply

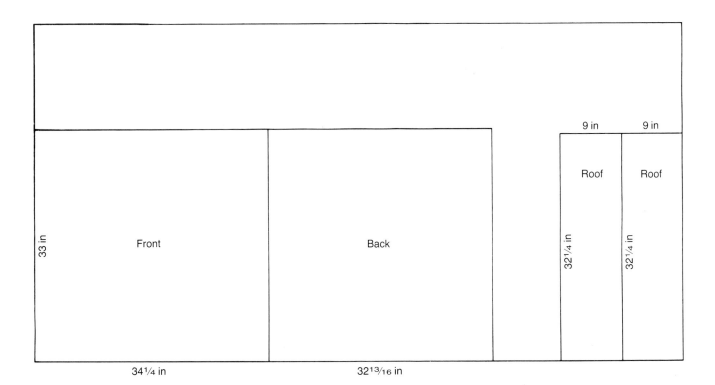

Fig 110 Cutting diagram

Before cutting the top corners off the Sides at a 30° angle, 3½ in (8.9 cm) down, 6¼ in (15.9 cm) across (Fig 111), check the width of the two blocks of softwood which will be used to build the chimney. If they are wider than the flat top of the Sides, reduce the height of the Sides to fit (Fig 112); if they are narrower, strip wood can be added during the construction.

Do not cut any opening in the Front until all details of the brickwork have been measured (see page 72).

Sand all the cut edges. Choose the best surface of the Floors; using a black biro, draw floorboards ½ in (12 mm) apart along the 12¼ in (33 cm) width (the rooms are 15¾ in (40 cm) deep). Seal with two or three coats of Georgian Oak acrylic satin varnish, rubbing down between coats. The landings should not be varnished until cut to size later, as the

sawcut would damage the edges. Tile or paint the kitchen floor to resemble flagstones.

Fill any blemishes in the other panels. Sand them smooth and paint both sides with vinyl primer. Paint the ceilings white matt. Prime all the walls, even if they are to be papered, as this seals the surface.

Mark the pilot holes, approximately 4 in (10.2 cm) apart and ³⁄₁₆ in (5 mm) from the cut edges. Drill from the sides to be joined, using a ³⁄₆₄ in (1 mm) bit.

If the house is to be wired for lighting, now is the time to drill holes and grooves for tape or wire (see page 96).

Paint the hall (Walls and Back) before assembly, or paper it before the stairs are fitted.

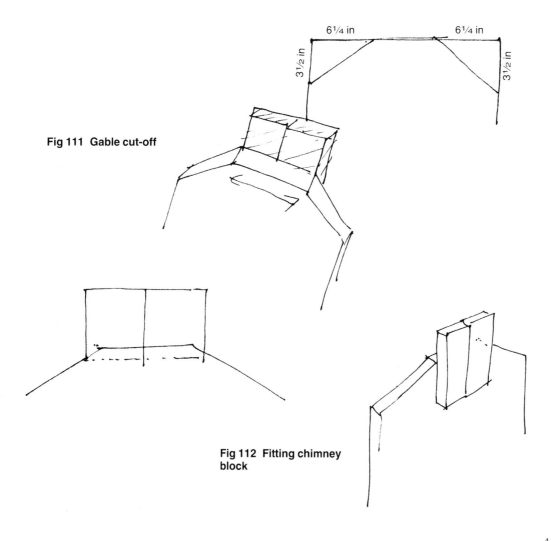

Fig 111 Gable cut-off

Fig 112 Fitting chimney block

A typical Georgian style town house of the 1840s

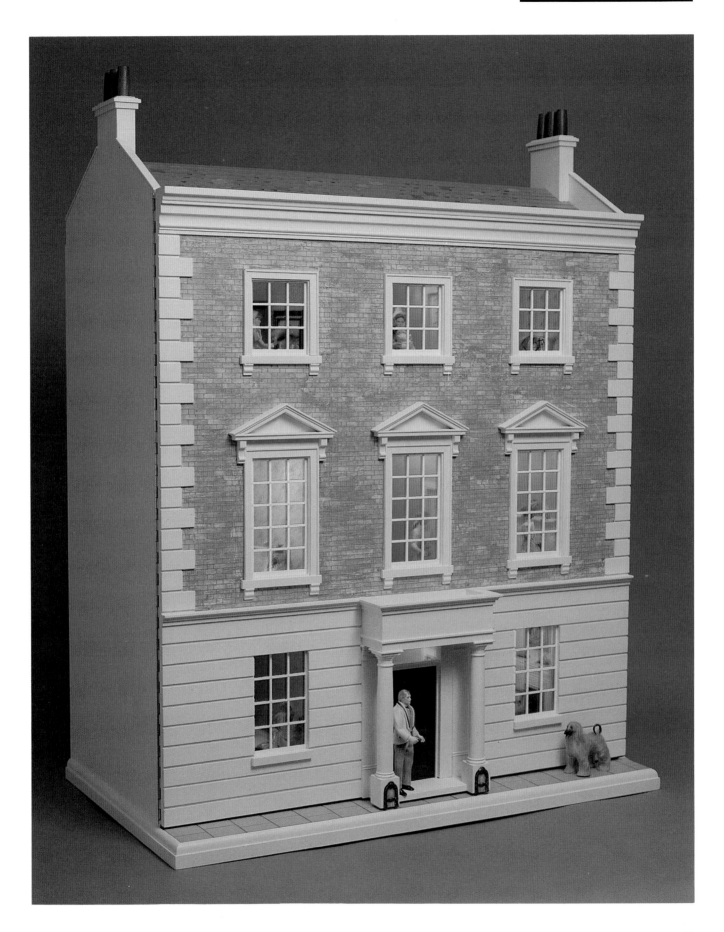

Diagram 6 SIX-ROOM HOUSE (i)

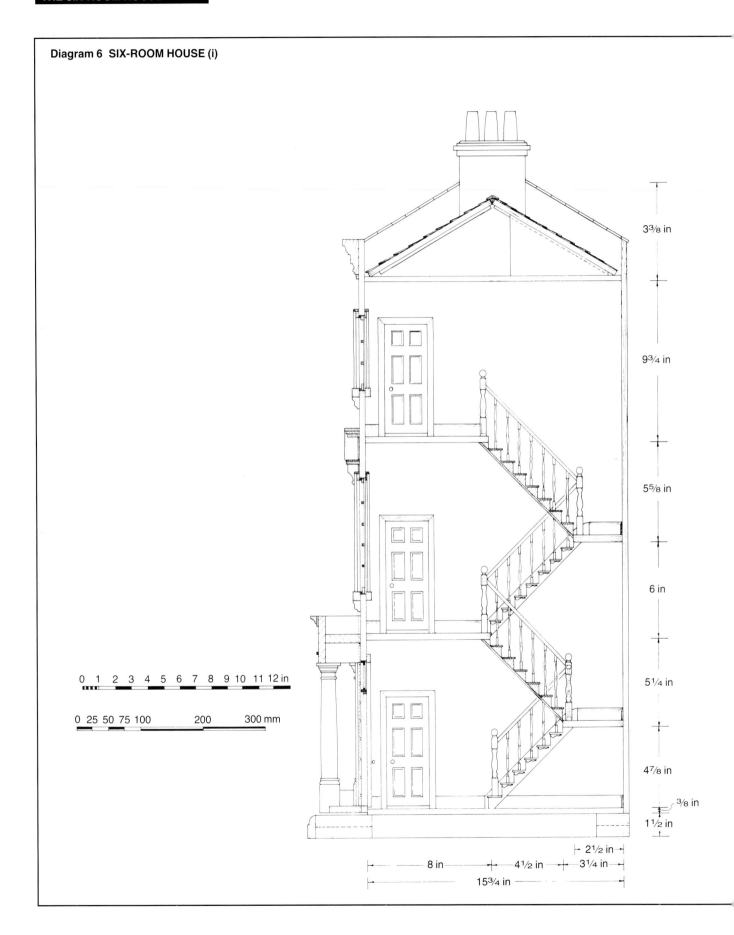

1¾ in

4½ in

4⅜ in

4¼ in

5⅝ in

6¾ in

4⅛ in

6 in

3⅛ in

1½ in

3⁄8 in   5½ in   3¾ in   5⅜ in   3¾ in   5⅜ in   3¾ in   5½ in

Diagram 6 SIX-ROOM HOUSE (ii)

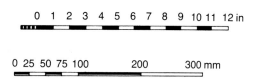

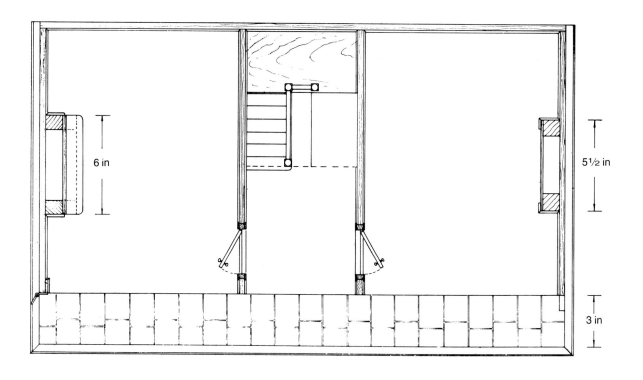

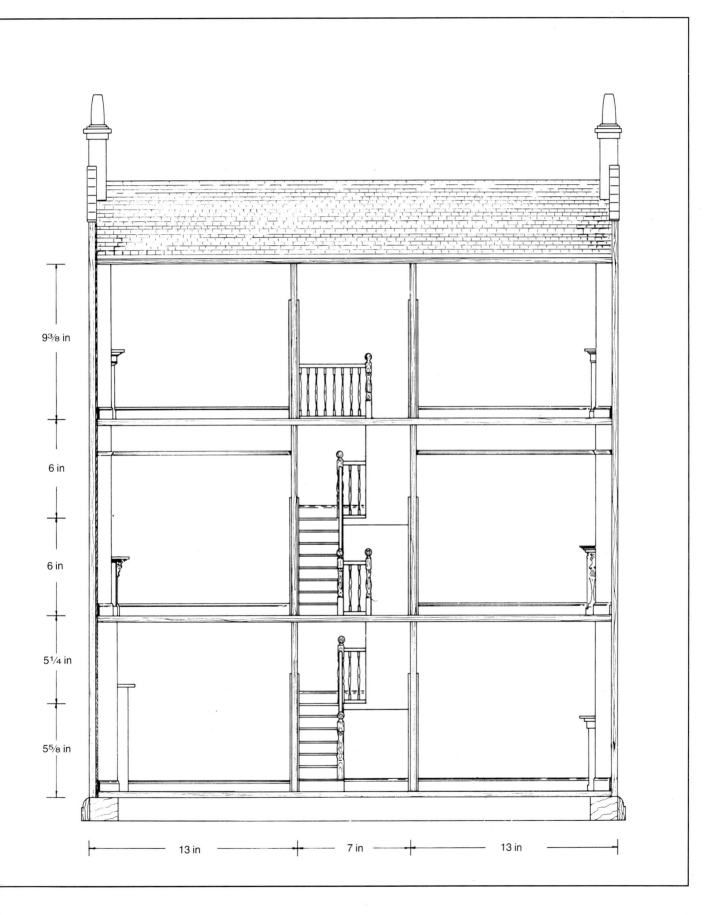

9³⁄₈ in

6 in

6 in

5¹⁄₄ in

5⁵⁄₈ in

13 in

7 in

13 in

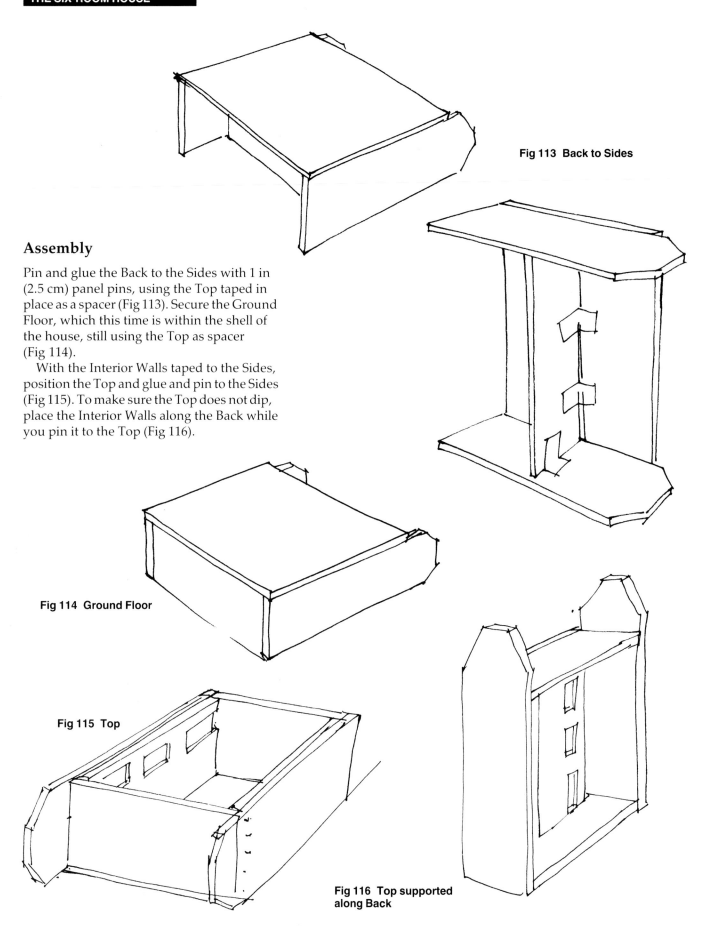

Fig 113 Back to Sides

Assembly

Pin and glue the Back to the Sides with 1 in (2.5 cm) panel pins, using the Top taped in place as a spacer (Fig 113). Secure the Ground Floor, which this time is within the shell of the house, still using the Top as spacer (Fig 114).

With the Interior Walls taped to the Sides, position the Top and glue and pin to the Sides (Fig 115). To make sure the Top does not dip, place the Interior Walls along the Back while you pin it to the Top (Fig 116).

Fig 114 Ground Floor

Fig 115 Top

Fig 116 Top supported along Back

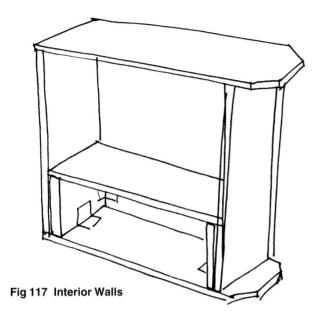

Fig 117 Interior Walls

Now position the Interior Walls, using the Floors as spacers top and bottom. Lay the house on its side and fix one Wall at a time (Fig 117). The other two floors can be used along the Back to keep the Wall straight.

If you use G-clamps to hold the top floors in place, you can work with the house upright (Fig 118). You will still need to turn it over to pin the Ground Floor.

Cut scrap spacers for the floors, four 10⅛ in (25.7 cm) and four 11¼ in (28.6 cm). Glue and pin, working upwards (Fig 119). Remember that the doorways may have been cut slightly below floor level.

Fig 118 With G-clamps

Fig 119 Spacers, Floors

Roof

Check that the centres of the flat top of the
Sides and Top coincide, then draw the
verticals.

Mark guidelines for the edge of the roof
³⁄₈ in (9 mm) in from the back and front of the
Top. The roof slope follows the line drawn
along the offcut from that edge to the centre
(Fig 120).

Cut four Roof supports from 1 in (2.5 cm)
square softwood to fit below the slope,
preferably cutting the ends to 30° and 60°
angles. If you do not have a set square, you
can mark off the angles by using scrapwood.
Hold the softwood below the guideline and
draw the horizontal along a piece of scrap
(Fig 121). When that angle has been cut, find
the vertical in the same way (Fig 122). Use the
first support as a guide for cutting the other
three.

Check that the Roof panels will fit, then
glue the supports to the Sides with a quick-
drying epoxy (i.e. two-part) glue, using the
triangles as support until it sets (Fig 123).
(Hammering pins could break the other
joints, unless pinned from the outside.)

Glue the offcut triangles over the Interior
Walls; you will see where they were pinned
(Fig 124). Fit a strip of wedge-shaped wood
between the supports, along the ³⁄₈ in (9 mm)
guidelines, to support the bottom edges of
the Roof (Fig 125).

Pin and glue the Back Roof. Then add the
Front Roof. To strengthen the ridge, glue a
length of dowel in the gap – ³⁄₈ in (9 mm)
should fit. This will be covered later by the
slates.

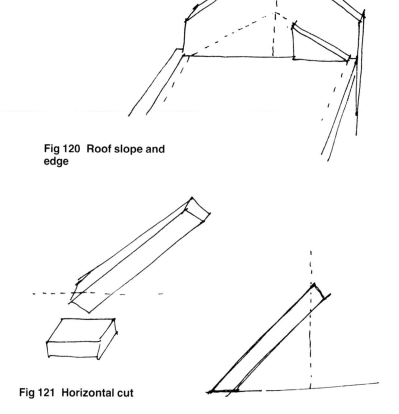

Fig 120 Roof slope and
edge

Fig 121 Horizontal cut

Fig 122 Vertical cut

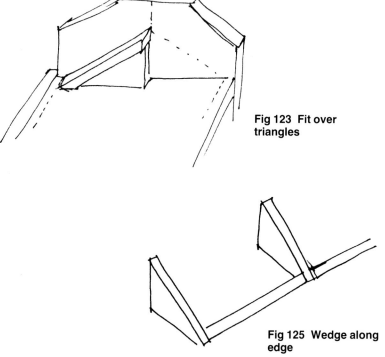

Fig 123 Fit over
triangles

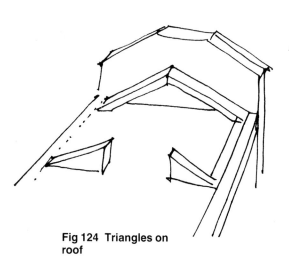

Fig 124 Triangles on
roof

Fig 125 Wedge along
edge

Chimneys

Each stack is built of two pieces of 2 in x 1 in (5.1 cm x 2.5 cm) softwood approximately 4½ in (11.5 cm) long, cut at 30° to match the roof slope, plus a panel of ⅜ in (9 mm) ply.

Measure where the top of the Side comes on the stack, and cut ⅜ in (9 mm) scrap to fit (Fig 126). (The softwood should have been checked against the flat top when that was cut; if the stack is too narrow, stripwood can be added; if too wide, fill in with scrap cut to the same angle (Fig 127).)

Glue and tape or pin the stacks together. When dry, add brick courses with ⅛ in x ¾ in (3 mm x 19 mm) and ⅛ in x ¼ in (3 mm x 6 mm).

Cut three 2 in (5.1 cm) chimney pots for each stack from ¾ in (19 mm) dowel, taper on a lathe, or simply rub down with sandpaper (Fig 128). (Ready-turned chimney pots are also available.) Drill and peg as before (see page 18). Paint the chimney pots red or terracotta before fitting. Do not fix the chimney stacks until the slates have been laid.

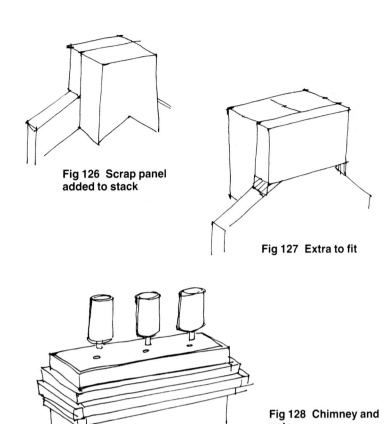

Fig 126 Scrap panel added to stack

Fig 127 Extra to fit

Fig 128 Chimney and pots

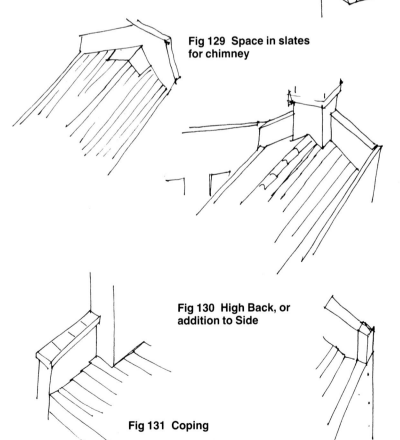

Fig 129 Space in slates for chimney

Fig 130 High Back, or addition to Side

Fig 131 Coping

Slates

Mark where the chimneys sit on the Roof, and lay layers of slates up to this line, starting from the bottom (Fig 129). See page 36 for instructions on laying tiles and slates.

To keep a smooth edge along the chimney, use card for the ridge tiles.

Unless the Back has been cut the same height as the Front, an extra piece of ⅜ in (9 mm) ply will need to be added to bring the top back edge of each Side out level with the Back (Fig 130).

Paint the exterior of the house cream and paint the chimney stacks *before* fitting. Leave an unpainted section on the Sides for gluing, paint the slates grey, then glue the chimneys in place.

Finish the Side slopes with ½ in x ⅛ in (12 mm x 3 mm) pre-painted coping (Fig 131).

Front

This will be hung on a piano hinge, so the inside of the left Side will need to be thickened by adding ¹⁄₁₆ in x ½ in (1.5 mm x 12 mm) (Fig 132). To cut the hinge to length, put it in a vice or hold it down with scrap wood near the cutting point (Fig 133). Use a hacksaw and put lubricating oil on the cut. File smooth.

Fit the hinge to the Side and Front (see page 19), remembering to fold the hinge inside out round the *outside* of the Side and Front for the position of the screws. Use ⅜ in (9 mm) no. 3 brass screws, and pilot with a ³⁄₃₂ (1.5 mm) in drill bit.

Once the screwholes are correctly positioned, you can remove the Front to start decorating it.

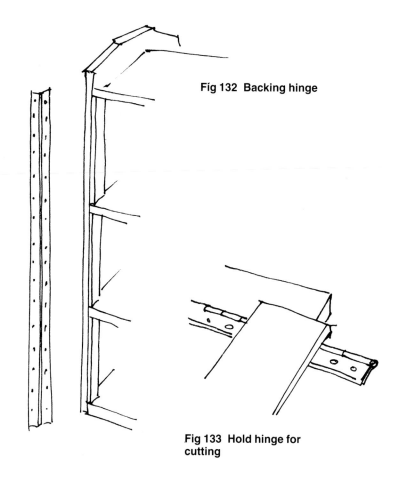

Fig 132 Backing hinge

Fig 133 Hold hinge for cutting

Windows and doorways

The windows, when lined, must line up with the rustication on the ground floor – 1 in (2.5 cm) with ⅛ in (3 mm) gap. Measure ten strips up, and allow space for your moulding, approximately ⅝ in (16 mm).

Draw the windows and doorway (Fig 134), drill and cut out. Line the cut edges of the windows with ⅛ in x ⅜ in (3 mm x 9 mm), flush with the outside, to retain the glazing bars. Cut the horizontals to full width, 3¾ in (9.5 cm), and the uprights to fit 5¾ in (14.6 cm), 6½ in (16.5 cm) and 4 in (10.2 cm). Line the sides and top of the doorway, with the verticals cut to the full height.

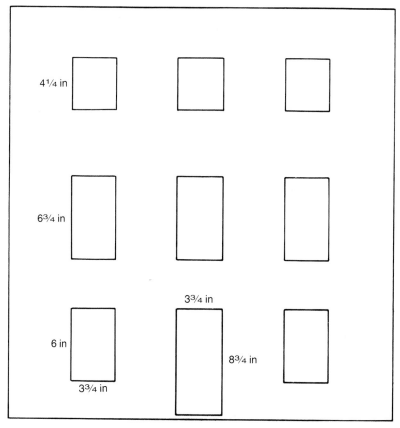

Fig 134 Cutting plan for windows and door

Porch

Cut ³⁄₈ in (9 mm) ply – front panel 7³⁄₄ in x 2³⁄₄ in (19.7 cm x 7 cm); sides 2¹⁄₈ in x 2³⁄₄ in (5.3 cm x 7 cm); centre 7 in x 2¹⁄₈ in (17.8 cm x 5.3 cm) – and glue and pin the canopy together as indicated (Fig 135). The top lines up with the top of the rustication cornice.

Lay the Front flat and glue on the canopy, weighting it until dry. If you prefer to screw it in place, drill pilot holes from the front as indicated (Fig 136). Screw from behind, using no. 4 countersunk steel screws ⁷⁄₈ in or ³⁄₄ in (23 mm or 19 mm).

Fix the step by the same method. Cut 6¹⁄₈ in x 1⁷⁄₈ in (15.5 cm x 4.8 cm). Cut out each end, ⁷⁄₁₆ in (11 mm) x ⁵⁄₈ in (15 mm) deep (Fig 137).

Cut 1¹⁄₂ in and 1¹⁄₄ in (3.8 cm and 3.2 cm) square capitals out of ¹⁄₈ in (3 mm) sheet for the top of each pillar. Drill ¹⁄₈ in (3 mm) centre holes for locating the pillars (Fig 138). Glue and pin, turning the Front upside down to support the canopy.

Build out the wall above and below the canopy with ³⁄₃₂ in (2.5 mm) sheet to match the rustication. Add 1¹⁄₄ in (3.2 cm) wide pilasters, and their 1⁵⁄₈ in (4.1 cm) high bases made from another layer of ³⁄₃₂ in (2.5 mm), cut to fit round the step. Cut two plinths, 1⁵⁄₈ in (4.1 cm) high, from 1¹⁄₂ in (3.8 cm) square planed softwood.

Attach the short walls that join the pilasters to the plinths, but do not fix the plinths yet: cut two ³⁄₈ in (9 mm) ply 1¹⁄₄ in (3.2 cm) high, and check that the depth is ¹⁵⁄₁₆ in (2.4 cm) (Fig 139).

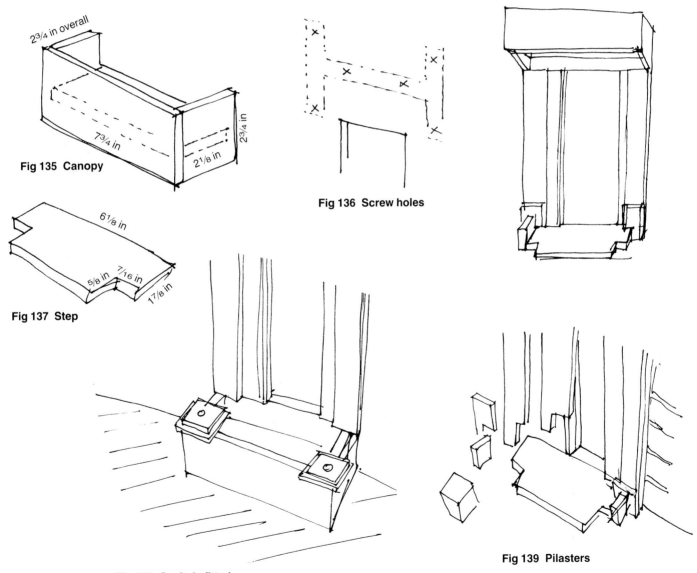

Fig 135 Canopy

Fig 136 Screw holes

Fig 137 Step

Fig 138 Capitals fitted

Fig 139 Pilasters

Check the height between plinth and capital – 7⅛ in (18 cm) – before cutting pillars from 1 in (2.5 cm) dowel or broom handle. If you cannot turn them yourself, find a local furniture maker or repairer or contact a specialist in doll's house turnings. Otherwise you can taper the pillars towards the top by rubbing them down with sandpaper, and bevelling the top. 'Rings' may be added with string or card, or built up with discs of different diameters – but only if you can match the centres (Fig 140).

Drill and peg the pillars top and bottom with ⅛ in (3 mm) dowel; drill matching holes in the plinths. Check that the pillars are upright when fitted before gluing them in place (Fig 141). Use G-clamps, if available, to hold the plinths, remembering to protect the surfaces with scrap wood before tightening the clamps, or tape and weight until dry.

The ground floor windows fit between the strips of rustication

Fig 140 Pillar

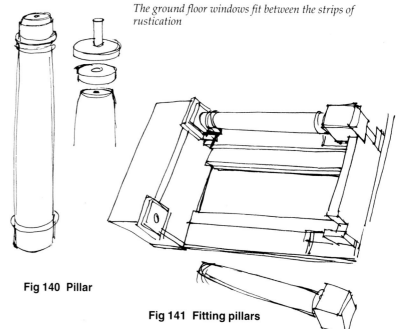

Fig 141 Fitting pillars

Stonework

Cut 1 in (25 mm) strips from $3/32$ in (2.5 mm) sheet for the rustication. Make sure they are cut to uniform lengths, approximately $12\frac{5}{8}$, $5\frac{5}{8}$ and $3\frac{1}{2}$ in (32.1, 14.3 and 8.9 cm) to overlap the window lining (Fig 142), but check your measurements first. The top strip can be cut wider to fit behind the moulding (Fig 143). Glue $\frac{1}{8}$ in (3 mm) apart.

Use contact adhesive, as a water-based glue can make thin wood swell and buckle unless it is very heavily weighted down.

Fit the moulding, about $\frac{5}{8}$ in (15 mm) high x $\frac{3}{8}$ in (9 mm) deep, above the top strip and around the top of the porch, mitring the joints. Add a $\frac{1}{8}$ in (3 mm) square strip $\frac{1}{2}$ in (1.2 cm) up from the bottom of the canopy (Fig 144). A

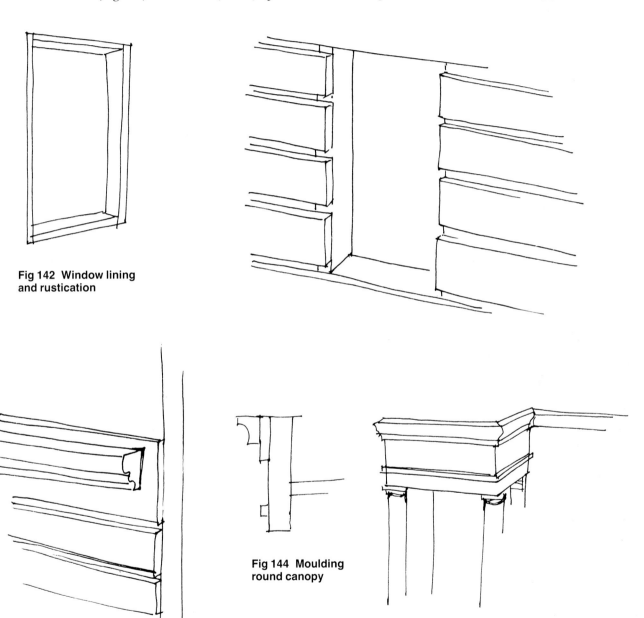

Fig 142 Window lining and rustication

Fig 143 Moulding over rustication

Fig 144 Moulding round canopy

small piece of moulding ³⁄₁₆ in (5 mm) wide will add a neat finish to the join between the pilaster and its base (Fig 145). Any turnings at the top of the pillar can be matched with small stripwood or moulding on the pilasters.

The quoins alternate, 2 in x 1 in (5.1 cm x 2.5 cm) and 1¼ in x 1 in (3.2 cm x 2.5 cm), starting from the bottom with the longer ones. On a detached house, the shorter ones extend farther round the corner (Fig 146); any addition to the sides would need cutting back near the hinge to allow the Front to open fully. Fit 18 strips ⅛ in (3 mm) apart, leaving approximately 2³⁄₈ in (6 cm) for the top moulding. This can be built up from several sections, using square and picture frame, dentil (a row of squares), and may extend above the Front (Fig 147).

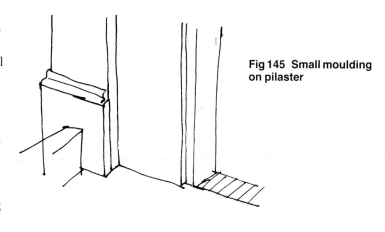

Fig 145 Small moulding on pilaster

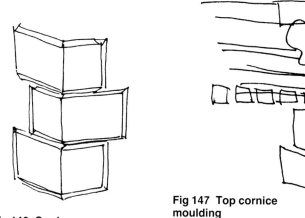

Fig 147 Top cornice moulding

Fig 146 Quoins

Windows (surround)

The architraves are built up from ⅜ in x ⅛ in (9 mm x 3 mm) and ³⁄₁₆ in x ⅛ in (5 mm x 3 mm). You can add further strips of ¹⁄₁₆ in (1.5 mm), or cut them from ½ in (12 mm) moulding. Overlap the join with the window lining by ¹⁄₁₆ in (1.5 mm), so that it becomes another layer in the moulding (Fig 148). Mitre the top corners. Fit the window sills, ½ in x ¼ in (12 mm x 6 mm), 5 in (12.7 cm) long, and 3¾ in (9.5 cm) on the ground floor.

The pediments are built up as illustrated (Fig 149), the top angle mitred at 60° and the sides at 30°. Cut two 3⅝ in (9.2 cm) lengths of ³⁄₃₂ in (2.5 mm) sheet to a depth of ¾ in (1.9 cm) for the top slopes of the pediment. Mitre at the top, but leave square at the overhanging ends. Support on a cross-piece, 6¼ in (15.9 cm) long, cut to a depth of ⅝ in (1.5 cm). Add a further ½ in x ¼ in (12 mm x 6 mm) strip below the cross-piece, 6⅛ in (15.5 cm) long. Support the slopes themselves with

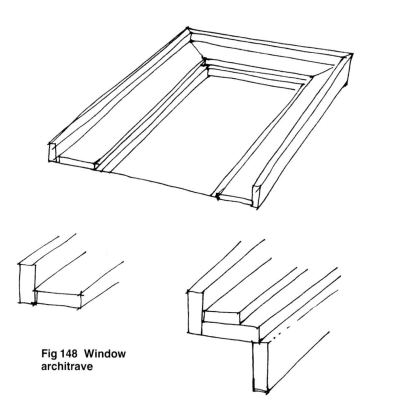

Fig 148 Window architrave

⅝ in (1.5 cm) deep ³⁄₃₂ in (2.5 mm) sheet, and a further ½ in x ¼ in (12 mm x 6 mm) strip, both mitred to fit within the triangle (Fig 149).

Cut brackets of moulding to support the window sills (they should line up with the architrave), and others to support the pediments ½ in (12 mm) above the architrave. (You can make them up from sections of several curves, or cut them out of layers of sheetwood.) Check that the pediments will fit level, but do not fix in place until the bricks are painted. Mark the position with a pencil line. (Biro or felt tip could bleed through when painted.) Paint all the 'stonework' cream, including the pediments and the strip of wall between their bracket supports.

Fig 149 Architrave and pediment

Brickwork

This can be treated as before (see page 35), with the mortar revealed by scraping through a darker colour. However, clean yellow bricks are almost the same colour as mortar, so this time a good colour match was achieved by stippling the acrylic varnish used on the

floors over a light pink acrylic base. Tint the vinyl primer with acrylic colours and test on scrap wood first.

The bricks, ¾ in x ⁹⁄₃₂ in (19 mm x 7.2 mm), should line up with the quoins. This is not too difficult to work out if you measure 1⅛ in (29 mm), halve it, then halve it again.

The mortar is drawn with a ruling pen, using grey paint. Keep the bevelled edge of your ruler or straightedge off the surface, to avoid paint flooding underneath. A grey felt tip pen is much easier to use, but the lines could fade with time.

Finish with a coat of clear matt vinyl varnish. Glue the pediments in place.

Windows (glazing)

Prepare stripwood for the window frames, ³⁄₁₆ in x ⅛ in (5 mm x 3 mm) for the sides and tops; ¼ in x ⅛ in (6 mm x 3 mm) for the bottom, and glazing bars, ⅛ in (3 mm) square. Prime, sand and finish with two coats of white vinyl silk before cutting to fit; cut away to half depth at the joints (see page 21). The windows are 3½ in (8.9 cm) wide x 5¾ in (14.6 cm), 6½ in (16.5 cm) and 4 in (10.2 cm) high. Glue the bars together, keeping the horizontals to the front. The windows can be taped to a flat surface until dry, but take care not to use too much glue, or they will stick there!

Fit the windows, and perspex or glass cut to size. Retain from inside with the architrave and window sills, cut to overlap by ⅛ in (3 mm), using the same construction as the exterior (Fig 150).

Fig 150 Glazing and retainer

Fig 151 Front Door

Front Door

Cut a panel of 1/16 in (1.5 mm) ply to 7 in x 3½ in (17.8 cm x 8.9 cm). Build up the door panelling with ½ in x 3/32 in (12 mm x 2.5 mm) strips on the sides and top, ¾ in (19 mm) across the bottom, 7/16 in (11 mm) for the two cross-pieces and the centre upright. Add raised panels of thin card or ply sheet cut ¾ in (19 mm) wide and cut to height within each door panel. Fine moulding can be used to edge the recesses (Fig 151).

Sand the edges of the centre panels before gluing. Prime, sand, fit the hinges and finish the door with gloss paint or modelmaker's enamel. Add any door furniture before hanging on the ¼ in x ½ in (6 mm x 12 mm) door surround. Cut ¼ in (6 mm) square to fit across the opening above the door, 7 1/16 in (18 cm) up, to hold the fanlight (Fig 152). Glue and fit the door surround (Fig 153). The top should overlap the fanlight to retain the glazing. Add a 1/8 in x 3/8 in (3mm x 9 mm) strip behind the cross-piece as a retainer (Fig 154) and 1/8 in (3 mm) square strips to retain each side if necessary. Fit the glass or plastic from the front, retaining with 1/8 in (3 mm) square strip. Use 1/16 in (1.5 mm) square stop round the door opening.

Fig 152 Cross-piece

Fig 153 Hanging door

Fig 154 Addition to cross-piece

Base

This is made from 2 in x 1½ in (5.1 cm x 3.8 cm) finished softwood, actually about ¼ in (6 mm) less. To bring it out to the depth of the porch, two widths are used across the front. Cut halving joints as shown (upside down) (Fig 155), glue and screw together using 1 in (2.5 cm) no. 6 countersunk screws. Turn the framework over so that the joints will be hidden under the house. Bevel the sides and front by adding simple moulding of the same height, mitred at the corners (Fig 156).

Screw the Base to the house; 1½ in (3.8 cm) no. 8 countersunk steel screws should be the right length, but check first that they are long enough to hold without coming up through the floor (Fig 157).

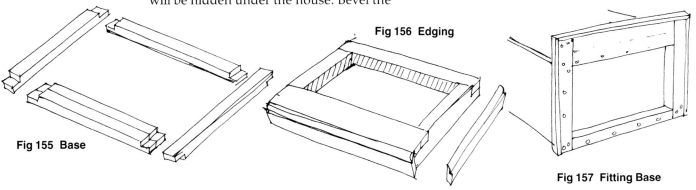

Fig 155 Base

Fig 156 Edging

Fig 157 Fitting Base

An elegant drawing room, with fine examples of British craftsmen's work, and American lighting

79

Stairs

Various kits are available, and made-up lengths can be cut shorter. The stairs, in multiples of ½ in (12 mm), ¾ in (19 mm), etc., can determine the height of the rooms. In this house, they have been built with ¾ in (19 mm) risers, rather high in real life (9 in/ 22.8 cm), but necessary to reach the height without making the house much deeper.

The strings this time support the treads, instead of enclosing them. The banisters peg into each tread and, as the hall is 7 in (18 cm) wide, there is a stairwell of about 1½ in (4 cm) between the flights.

Most real staircases have a newel post only at the bottom, and the handrail curves round the landings. However, it is easier to build a straight banister, with posts top and bottom. If you cannot buy ready-turned newel posts, use ⅜ in (9 mm) square, ⅛ in (3 mm) square or dowel in place of banisters, and three strips of wood (see page 31) for the handrail.

Cut the stepped strings as shown (Fig 158), two pairs for the ground floor to fit 10½ in (26.7 cm) height floor to floor (14 steps) and two pairs to join the upper floors with a 12 in (30.5 cm) height (16 steps). These can be cut from ⅛ in (3 mm) or thicker, ¹³⁄₁₆ in (2 cm) wide. The lower pairs are 7½ in (19.1 cm) long. Cut the four strips together. The first step will be 1⅛ in (2.8 cm) high x ¾ in (19 mm), and the remaining five ¾ in (19 mm), with a short top step ⅜ in (9 mm) to fit below the landing. The ground floor step is trimmed square to ¾ in (19 mm) – on other flights this will butt against the landing. The top pairs are 8⅝ in (21.9 cm) long, cut to give one high step, six ¾ in (19 mm) and one ⅜ in (9 mm). Use ³⁄₃₂ in (2.5 mm) for the inner string, or the same thickness as the skirting. Cut 1⅛ in (2.9 cm) wide and approximately 7½ in and 8½ in (19 cm and 21.5 cm) long. Square off the ground floor, cutting the vertical level with the tread, or curve it to meet the skirting. Curve or cut square on the landings, and cut away to fit. Check they match the stepped strings. If you wish, the sides of the string can be decorated with thin slices of moulding below each tread. Cut 30 risers ⅝ in x 2⅝ in (16 mm x 6.7 cm) and 26 treads 1 in x 2¾ in (2.5 cm x 7 cm), ³⁄₃₂ in (2.5 mm) thick. If you want to varnish the stairs, do so before the strips are cut to length, on one side only, to avoid marking them with glue. Drill treads to fit the banisters ⅜ in

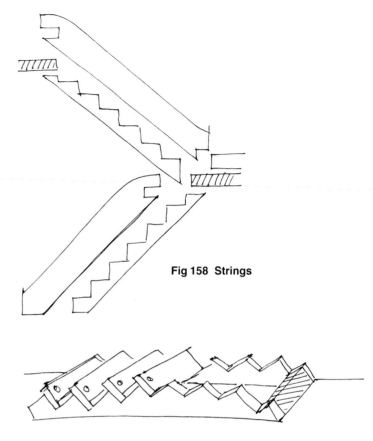

Fig 158 Strings

Fig 159 Treads and riser

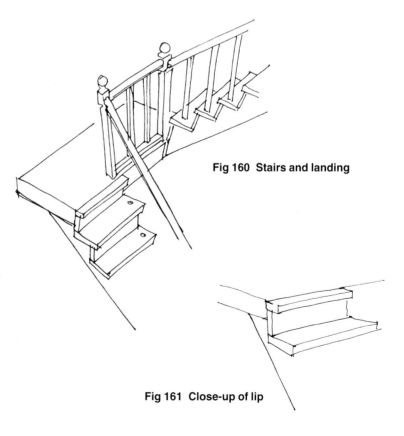

Fig 160 Stairs and landing

Fig 161 Close-up of lip

(9 mm) from the front edge, 3/16 in (5 mm) from the side. (A square peg *will* fit in a round hole!) The outside corner can be rounded. Tape the lefthand string to scrap to make a stop when fitting, and glue spacers top and bottom (Fig 159). Glue the treads and risers in position.

The top step of each flight has been cut short to incorporate the 3/8 in (9 mm) landing (Fig 160). The lip must be added above the riser to match the other steps (Fig 161).

The front landings are 7 in wide x 8 in deep (17.8 cm x 20.3 cm), the half landing on the first flight is 3¼ in (8.2 cm) deep, deeper than the upper half landing (2½ in/6.3 cm) to allow for the extra step in that flight.

The front edges of the strings should line up with the landing (Fig 162) if you wish to keep the handrail/newel post joints level. The banisters on the landings will need to be raised on a strip of approximately ⅛ in x ¼ in (3 mm x 6 mm), or ¼ in (6 mm) square if you drill locating holes. This is because the banisters on a slope meet the newel posts at a different height because of their extra width (Fig 163). Try fitting the staircase together before you cut the depth of the front landings and handrail lengths.

Fit the banisters and handrail. (They may fit together without using much masking tape.) The height of the newel post is determined by its distance from the riser. If you trim the tops of the banisters to fit the

handrail angle, the newels must be shortened, or the bottom one moved nearer and the top farther away. Their position on the landings is determined by finding a middle point suitable for both flights, which is likely to be about ½ in (12 mm) back from the edge of the landing.

If the lower handrail comes too low, it will have to be joined at a lower point. If it is too high, add a horizontal section of handrail (Fig 164).

The bottom newel can be positioned against the first or second step or, very correctly, cut into the bottom step while resting on the ground floor, but this will make the banisters shorter. If you find it easier to rest the bottom step of each flight on the landing, another ¾ in (19 mm) will have to be added to the front landings. To keep the 3½ in (8.8 cm) newel posts level on the landing, the banisters on the flights have to be shortened from 2⅝ in (6.7 cm) to about 2¼ in (5.7 cm), and those on the landings built up to about 3⅝ in (9.2 cm). It is easier to let the handrail join where it will on the bottom newel and cut the bottom newels shorter, instead of into the step.

Having decided which method you will use, cut the landings to size. (They must fit *exactly* between the Interior Walls.) Make sure the direction of the grain matches the floors. Rule the floorboards with a black biro and apply coloured varnish as on the floors. The undersides should be matt white, as for the ceilings. Glue in position, using spacers, 10⅛ in (25.7 cm) and 11¼ in (28.5 cm). The half-landings need 4⅞ in (12.5 cm) and 10⅞ in (27.7 cm). Cornice moulding will give added support to the front landings.

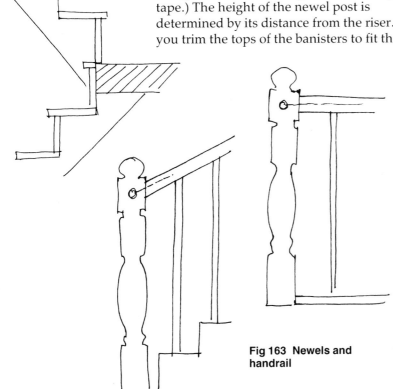

Fig 162 Line up flights

Fig 163 Newels and handrail

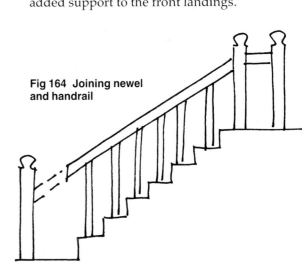

Fig 164 Joining newel and handrail

Paint the stairs white, except the surfaces to be glued. It may be best to paint the banisters in position if they are already a tight fit.

Assemble each flight as indicated (Fig 165). The newels can be drilled to take ⅛ in (3 mm) locating pegs. Fit the landing banisters together with the top newel and bottom rail. Check that the locating pegs in the newels fit with the next flight.

The Walls and the Back of the Hall must be decorated before fitting the staircase.

Paint and glue the skirtings on the landings, and the wall strings down the Side Walls. (Leave a ¼ in (6 mm) strip unpainted at the bottom of the strings for gluing.) Check the angle first by drawing down the back of each flight, and cut away the wallpaper to the depth of the wall string. If the walls are painted, key the surface by scraping with a knife to give a matt finish. Glue with epoxy resin for a firm joint. Brace with scrap strip if necessary.

Cut panels of 1/16 in (1.5 mm) ply or sheet to finish the underside of each flight. The first flight is 7 in x 2¹¹/₁₆ in (17.8 cm x 6.8 cm), the return 7½ in x 2¹¹/₁₆ in (19 cm x 6.8 cm), the middle floor 8 in x 2¹¹/₁₆ in (20.3 cm x 6.8 cm) and the return 8½ in x 2¹¹/₁₆ in (21.6 cm x 6.8 cm). Check the size before cutting. Prime and paint matt white to match the ceilings, but do not fit until the stairs are glued in place.

Start with the bottom flight, using epoxy resin. Brace with strips until dry. Do not use masking tape on the walls as it could mark the new paint or wallpaper.

When the stairs are firmly in place, finish the underside with the white panels.

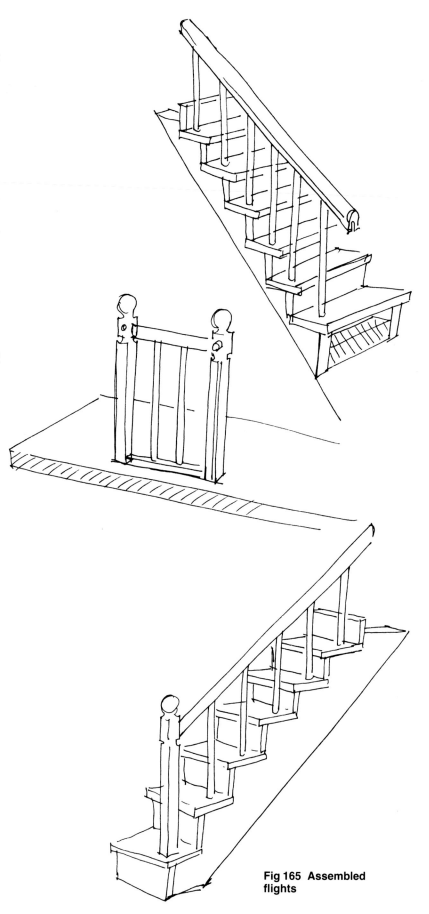

Fig 165 Assembled flights

You can find a miniature version of almost anything, from the family silver laid out in the dining room, to the Visitor's book in the hall, to the antique paintings and Staffordshire pottery

Chimney breasts

These are optional, but do make a more realistic space for your fireplaces. A firebasket can be positioned correctly behind the fire-surround, instead of protruding dangerously into the room. Choose your fireplaces first, unless you are making you own, so that the openings can be cut to fit and the chimney breasts made wide enough.

Cut panels of ⅛ in (3 mm) ply to fit the floor-to-ceiling heights and appropriate widths. For the top floor, cut two 9⅜ in x 4½ in (23.8 cm x 11.4 cm), for the middle floor two 11¼ in x 5½ in (28.5 cm x 14 cm), for the ground floor one 10⅛ in x 5½ in (25.7 cm x 14 cm), and one 3⅞ in x 6 in (9.8 cm x 15.2 cm) to fit above the kitchen range.

Trace the inside of the fireplaces and cut openings to fit. Back the panels with two battens of 1 in (2.5 cm) square softwood cut to height. If you wish to line the openings, cut more softwood to fit either side (Fig 166).

The fireplace in the kitchen should be made to fit a built-in range exactly. This one takes a 4⅛ in (10.5 cm) width.

Cut two 6¼ in (15.9 cm) lengths of 2 in x 1 in (5.1 cm x 2.5 cm) softwood for the sides and one 4⅛ in (10.5 cm) for the top. Use 4⅛ in (10.5 cm) of ⅛ in (3 mm) ply or sheet cut to the same depth for the base (Fig 167). If you wish to raise the range from the floor, this could be thicker. You would then need to use 1 in (2.5 cm) for the top, to allow space for the chimney.

Add 1 in (2.5 cm) wide strips of 3/16 in (5 mm) each side, cut to a ceiling height of 10⅛ in (27.7 cm). Cover the front with the panel of ⅛ in (3 mm) ply 3⅞ in high x 6 in wide (9.8 cm x 15.2 cm). Cut the mantlepiece from a strip of 3/16 in x ½ in (5 mm x 12 mm) to the full width, 6 in (15.2 cm). Check this is deep enough to take any pans or jugs you intend to place there (Fig 168).

A fitted range may have cast iron panels lining the fireplace above the cooking surface, in which case paint the interior black. Otherwise 'whitewash' with soot stains will show up your range and pans better.

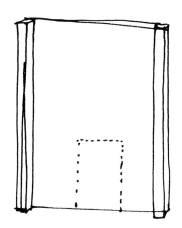

Fig 166 Chimney breast

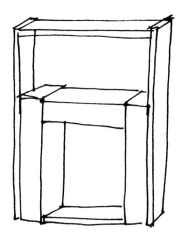

Fig 167 Kitchen chimney breast

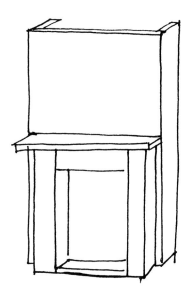

Fig 168 Kitchen, with mantlepiece

Decorating

Prime and sand the doors and skirtings, and any cornice and picture rails. Finish with white silk emulsion, and fit the doorknobs.

All walls should have been primed before assembly and the ceilings painted matt white. The wiring should have been finished and hidden in the ceilings, behind the skirtings, etc. (see page 96).

Paint any unfinished fireplaces (as in the kitchen) before fitting, and paint the interior of the chimney breasts black. Hearths of grey (stone) or marbled paper can be cut to fit the size of the fenders, but this is easy to do later if you have not yet chosen them.

If you paper the rooms before adding mouldings, cut the wallpaper a little short to leave a firm gluing surface. Cut the wallpaper to size and try in position before pasting. One piece *can* fit round the chimney breast and to the back wall, but it is easier to make a join behind the chimney. The wallpaper should overlap at a join as any inaccurate cutting would expose the primer. Make sure the patterns match; you may need to cut away almost a whole repeat.

Use wallpaper paste, as it will not stain the paper and is easier to remove when re-decorating. Paint a thick solution on both walls and paper, and leave a couple of minutes as the paper will stretch when wet. If it becomes too dry, apply another coat before positioning.

Starting from the front, press the wallpaper firmly into the near side of the chimney breast, using a small set square, 6 in (15 cm) plastic ruler or 3 in (7.6 cm) piece of card – nothing too sharp that might tear the paper. Wipe away any excess glue in the corner, then continue round the chimney breast. Paper the rest of that wall before overlapping on the far side of the chimney.

To make sure the pattern is continuous, paper the back wall and the internal wall last, overlapping the joins (Fig 169).

If you are papering a room after the door is fitted, leave extra paper and slit into the corners so that the excess can be folded back. Cut along the fold with scissors, or leave to dry and slice with a sharp craft knife.

The imported doors come ready-pinned to a framework which fits the doorway, with the architrave already attached on one surface and three strips to be fitted on the other side (see page 60, Fig 109). The fixed side should be in the hall, so that the door opens into the room. The shorter panels are at the bottom. If you wish to hang the doors on the right to open correctly into the room and away from the corner, you will have to remove the strip under the door, unpin from the top and re-pin to hang the other side, or use small brass hinges.

If you are pinning into the floor, instead of the step, drill a longer hole than necessary in the bottom of the door to take the pin. Hold the pin up with a knife blade until the door is in position, then let the pin drop into the hole.

All skirtings, cornices and picture rails must be mitred if they are moulded. Brace them with a strip of wood while the glue is drying. Use a light glue if you are running wire behind the skirting, so that it is removable. The grander the room, the more complicated the mouldings can be. The kitchen does not need a skirting, but it gives a neat finish to the room.

Plaster ceiling roses can be used to hang the centre lights, whether electrified or not. Anaglypta (embossed) paper makes excellent ceiling mouldings. The pattern should be centred on the light fitting, and it will also hide the electric wiring. I have even seen paper doilies cut down to represent fine ceiling moulding.

One reason I like a white staircase is that it shows off a stair carpet so well. If you cannot find special doll's house carpet, use braid, velvet ribbon or felt cut to size. Glue it down with wallpaper paste or a few dabs of light glue; petroleum-based glues tend to discolour.

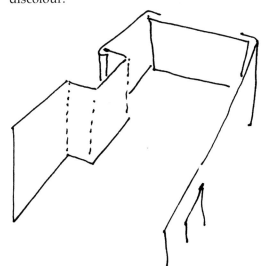

Fig 169 Wallpaper

This nursery is full of appealing toys – a jointed teddy, a splendid rocking horse, picture books – and a doll's house!

Wallpaper paste or starch is useful to stop fabric fraying. This avoids those clumsy turnings that always ruin the scale of a doll's house, if you do not mind a permanently draped curtain. Soak the curtain in paste, arrange in the folds you want, and leave to dry on a flat surface. Alternatively, spray with starch when in position. The curtain can be glued or tacked behind a pelmet.

If you prefer soft curtains which you can pull, use very fine silk or Liberty lawn, or specialist American fabric. Antique doll's houses often have a knitting needle pushed through the top turning, held with a screw eye at each end. You can also use dowel or the special brass rods and rings now available.

To finish the exterior of the house, paint the doorstep matt white. The maid will spend an hour every morning hearthstoning it!

An easy way to indicate paving stones is to paste grey art paper to fit the flat part of the base, and rule lines with grey and brown felt tip pens, 1½ in (3.8 cm) apart, and 1½ in (3.8 cm) and 2 in (5.1 cm) from the back.

Now you have a desirable town residence, and all you need to do is furnish it!

*A fully furnished house takes on a life of its own,
particularly once the family moves in and the lights are lit*

THE BOX SHOP

This is a one-room plywood box 18 in wide x 10 in deep x 9¾ in high (45.7 cm x 25.4 cm x 24.8 cm), with a drop-in clear perspex top and a hinged shopfront 2½ in (6.4 cm) deep with a recessed entrance.

Cut panels of ⅜ in (9 mm) plywood as indicated (Fig 170). Draw floorboards ½ in (12 mm) apart with a black biro, then seal the Floor with an acrylic stain varnish. Use acrylic primer on all the other surfaces, and finish the inside Walls with two coats of vinyl matt emulsion.

Drill pilot holes about 4 in (10 cm) apart and ³⁄₁₆ in (5 mm) from the cut edge. Using 1 in (2.5 cm) panel pins and PVA white wood glue, pin and glue the Back to the Floor (Fig 171), allowing the Back to overhang by ⅛ in (3 mm). (You could pin ⅛ in (3 mm) square strip along the edge as a stop.) The other side of the Back will need supporting as usual, with scrap spacer taped in position or a pile of books to the correct height.

Place the box on its side, and fit the Side panels in turn (Fig 172), once again over-hanging the Floor by ⅛ in (3 mm). As the Front has to swing clear of the ground, this will raise the Floor to the level of the step outside.

Fit a Front Bar of planed 1½ in x 1 in (3.8 cm x 2.5 cm) softwood, 17¼ in (43.8 cm) long, to keep the box rigid. Pin and glue, making sure it fits square (Fig 173).

When all the joints are set firmly, glue a retaining strip for the drop-in panel just below the top edge of the Walls and Front Bar. The depth depends on the thickness used – here it is set down ¼ in (6 mm) to take ⁵⁄₃₂ in (4 mm) perspex. If you are using moulding, mitre the corners, but ¼ in (6 mm) square will do as well (Fig 174). Perspex can be cut to size by a glass or plastics merchant – take the box for an exact fit. If the edges are not polished, rub them down yourself with diminishing grades of wet and dry abrasive paper, finishing with 600 grit or finer.

Fit a strip of ¹⁄₁₆ in x ¼ in (1.5 mm x 6 mm) inside the left side to take the width of the piano hinge.

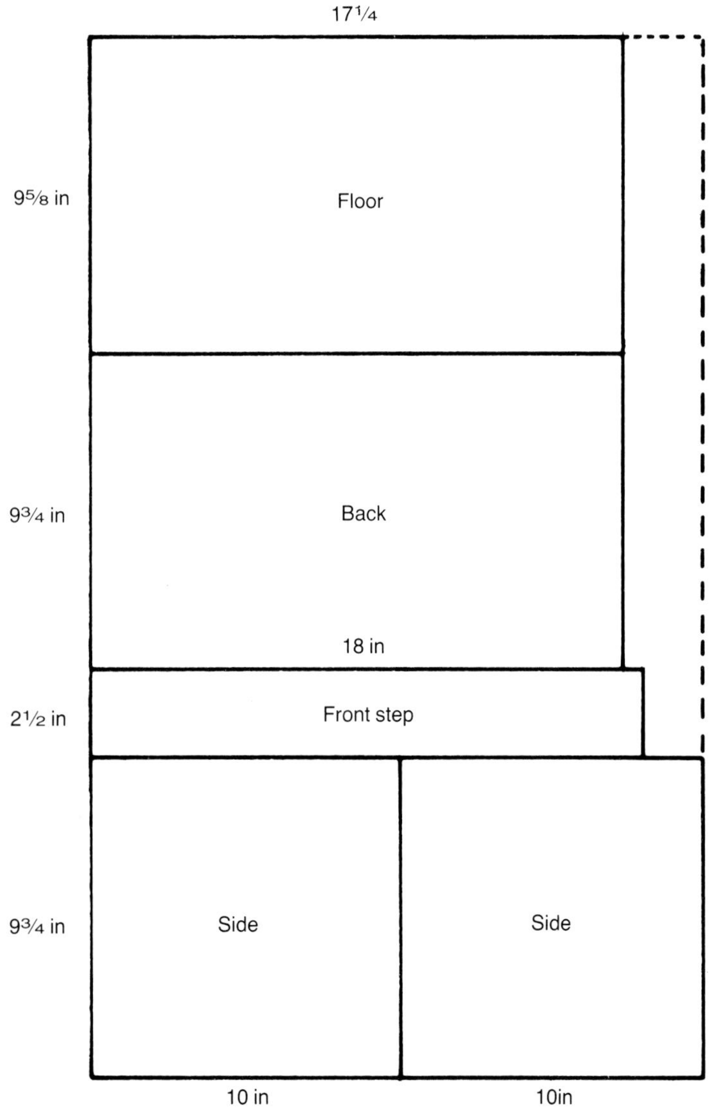

Fig 170 Cutting diagram

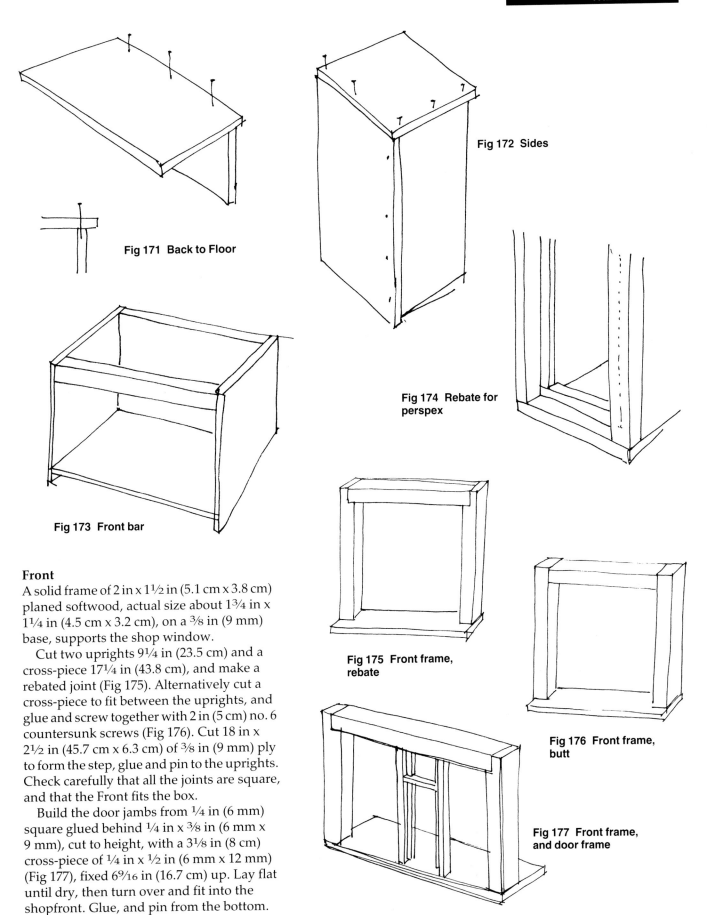

Fig 171 Back to Floor

Fig 172 Sides

Fig 173 Front bar

Fig 174 Rebate for perspex

Fig 175 Front frame, rebate

Fig 176 Front frame, butt

Fig 177 Front frame, and door frame

Front

A solid frame of 2 in x 1½ in (5.1 cm x 3.8 cm) planed softwood, actual size about 1¾ in x 1¼ in (4.5 cm x 3.2 cm), on a ⅜ in (9 mm) base, supports the shop window.

Cut two uprights 9¼ in (23.5 cm) and a cross-piece 17¼ in (43.8 cm), and make a rebated joint (Fig 175). Alternatively cut a cross-piece to fit between the uprights, and glue and screw together with 2 in (5 cm) no. 6 countersunk screws (Fig 176). Cut 18 in x 2½ in (45.7 cm x 6.3 cm) of ⅜ in (9 mm) ply to form the step, glue and pin to the uprights. Check carefully that all the joints are square, and that the Front fits the box.

Build the door jambs from ¼ in (6 mm) square glued behind ¼ in x ⅜ in (6 mm x 9 mm), cut to height, with a 3⅛ in (8 cm) cross-piece of ¼ in x ½ in (6 mm x 12 mm) (Fig 177), fixed 6⁹⁄₁₆ in (16.7 cm) up. Lay flat until dry, then turn over and fit into the shopfront. Glue, and pin from the bottom.

W. J. CALLOWAY

The width of the shop window can vary slightly with the width of the planed softwood, so you may have to adjust the length of the window sills and spacers and the width of the windows, or keep the front window the same as the diagram and alter the angle to the door.

Spacers top and bottom and sandwiched round the windowsills keep the whole structure straight. Cut eight spacers and two windowsills from ³⁄₃₂ in (2.3 mm) sheet, to fit exactly between the sides and the door jamb (Fig 178). The sill projects to the front of the jamb.

The spacers are 1½ in (3.8 cm) deep x 4⅞ in (12.4 cm) to the front corner; the sills are 1⅞ in (4.8 cm) deep x 5⅛ in (13 cm); and the full lengths are 5¹⁵⁄₁₆ in (15.1 cm) and 6³⁄₁₆ in (15.7 cm). The sill is cut to fit in front of the door jamb. The full lengths and the angle to the door may vary with the width of the softwood sides.

The delivery bicycle adds the finishing touch to this delightful grocer's shop

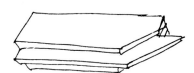

Fig 178 Front with sills and spacers

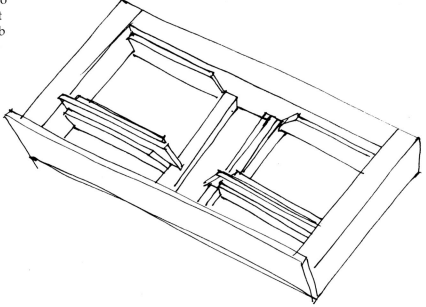

Diagram 7 BOX SHOP

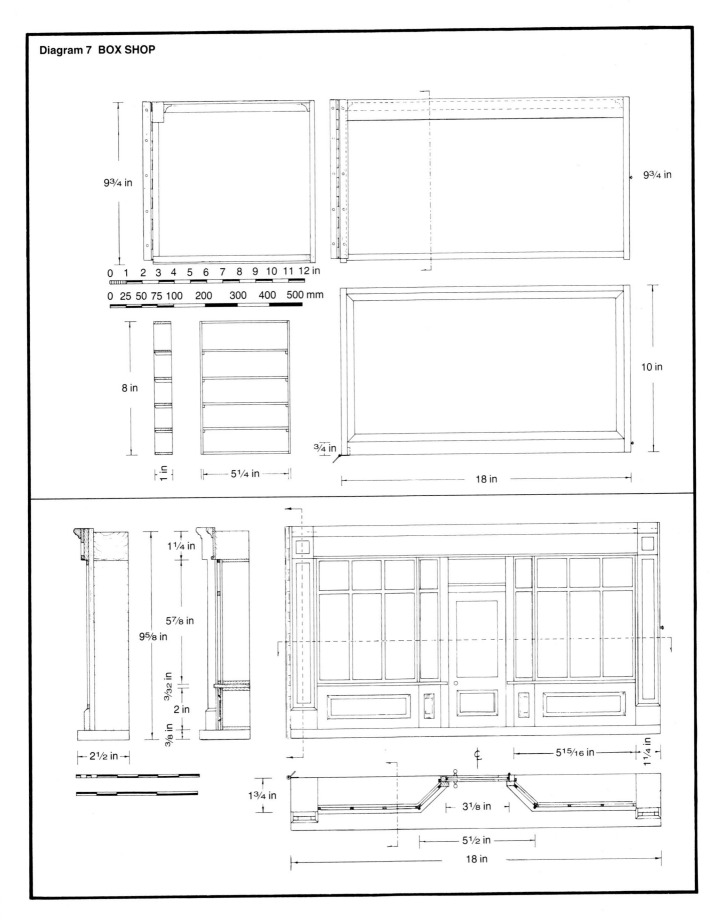

9³⁄₄ in

9³⁄₄ in

0 1 2 3 4 5 6 7 8 9 10 11 12 in

0 25 50 75 100 200 300 400 500 mm

8 in

10 in

³⁄₄ in

1 in

5¹⁄₄ in

18 in

1¹⁄₄ in

5⁷⁄₈ in

9⁵⁄₈ in

³⁄₃₂ in

2 in

³⁄₈ in

2¹⁄₂ in

1³⁄₄ in

3¹⁄₈ in

5¹⁵⁄₁₆ in

1¹⁄₄ in

5¹⁄₂ in

18 in

Glue spacers above and below the sills, tape and weight down to prevent warping. Glue top and bottom spacers while the Front is laid flat. Cut 2 in (5.1 cm) high shopboards to fit against the spacers from $\frac{1}{16}$ in (1.5 mm) sheet or ply (Fig 179), and build up with $\frac{3}{32}$ in (2.3 mm) strip, $\frac{3}{8}$ in (9 mm) wide for the top bar and $\frac{1}{2}$ in (12 mm) for the uprights and bottom bar (Fig 180). The front panels are $4\frac{13}{16}$ in (12.2 cm) wide and the sides approximately $1\frac{1}{2}$ in (3.8 cm).

More detail may be added with a centre raised panel of $\frac{1}{16}$ in (1.5 mm) sheet or even thinner card, set in $\frac{1}{4}$ in (6 mm) from the 'frame', and a small moulding to edge the 'frame' (Fig 181).

Cut and sand the parts for the panels. The uprights that meet at an angle will need to be mitred; sand back one edge. Glue down the centre panels, prime and sand before gluing the 'frame'. If you are painting these panels and the frame in two colours, you may prefer to paint the strips before gluing. Prime both sides first to avoid warping, then paint the finished colour on one side only. The small moulding must be painted before cutting and fitting.

Paint the step before gluing the shopboards in place. Use either the same matt white as the interior walls, to indicate 'hearthstone' again, or a very light grey or beige, for untreated stone.

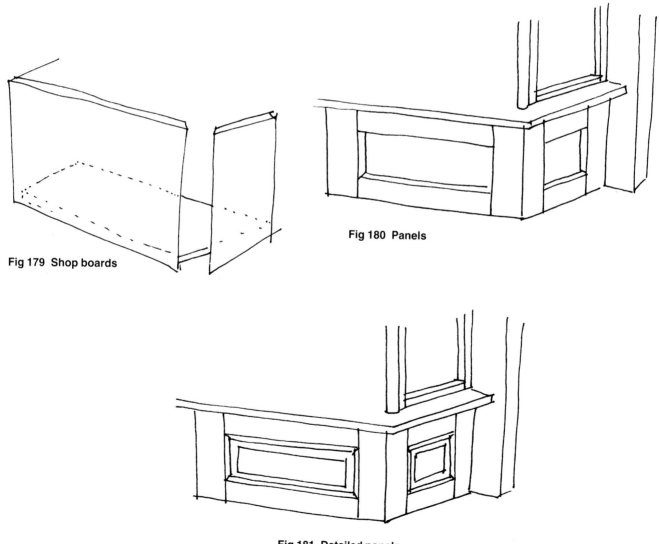

Fig 179 Shop boards

Fig 180 Panels

Fig 181 Detailed panels

The windows are built up with perspex or plastic sheet (use up to $1/16$ in (1.5 mm) thick), held top and bottom against the spacers by a window frame and glazing bars (Fig 182). The windows are $1^3/8$ in wide x $4^1/8$ in (3.5 cm x 10.5 cm), with smaller panels above $1^1/4$ in (3.2 cm) and glazing bars $1/8$ in (3 mm) square with a wider strip of $1/8$ in x $1/4$ in (3 mm x 6 mm) along the bottom. Make cut-away joints as before. Check that the windows fit between the spacers. Cut pieces of cardboard to check the position of the perspex and work out measurements for the angled windows (Fig 183). Cut two lengths of $1/8$ in (3 mm) dowel to height, to cover the angle between the windows (Fig 184). Paint all the strips and interior of the shop window before gluing together.

The $6^1/2$ in x 3 in (16.5 cm x 7.6 cm) door is built up with $1/2$ in x $3/32$ in (12 mm x 2.3 mm) strips over a centre panel of $1/16$ in (1.5 mm), but instead of being one sheet this is part perspex or clear acrylic sheet. The strips are wider than the sides of the centre panel, so overlap the perspex and keep it in place (Fig 185). They can be painted like the shopboards before assembly.

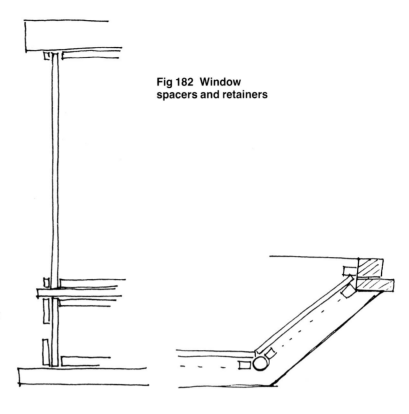

Fig 182 Window spacers and retainers

Fig 183 Top view

Fig 184 Dowel at corner joint

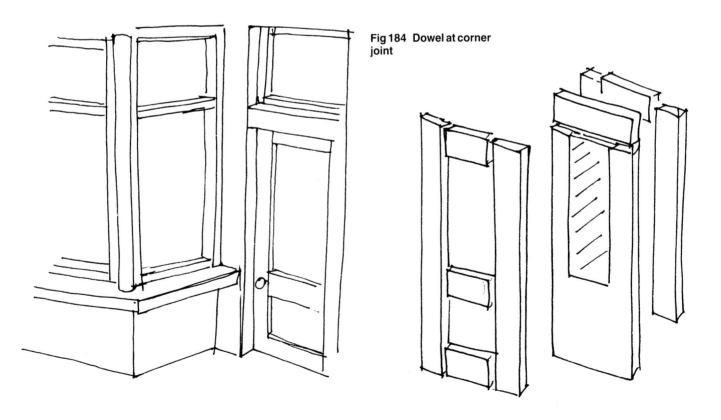

Fig 185 Shop door

93

The fanlight is retained inside and out with ⅛ in (3 mm) square.

The pilasters at the sides are built up with layers of ⅛ in (3 mm) (Fig 186). The bottom panel can be built out, with its top chamfered. Paint the dark strips and light panels before assembling. Cut a ⅛ in (3 mm) signboard to fit the depth of the top bar, plus any extra needed to fit behind the top moulding. Paint and letter (use Letraset) before fixing; remember to leave space for moulding and ⅛ in (3 mm) trim along the bottom to match that on the pilasters.

You can stock a general store with all sorts of goods; fruit and vegetables, garden tools, wickerwork, ironing boards, pots and pans . . . .

Fig 186 Pilasters

Hang the Front on a piano hinge, cut to length (see page 72). Build the counters and shelves (Fig 187), and start stocking the shop.

The counter is built of $\frac{1}{16}$ in (1.5 mm) sheet or ply, $9\frac{3}{4}$ in x 3 in (24.8 cm x 7.6 cm) with $\frac{1}{2}$ in (12 mm) strips, plus a kicking strip $\frac{1}{4}$ in (6 mm) high, and a top $\frac{1}{8}$ in (3 mm) thick. The three sets of shelving are cut from $\frac{3}{32}$ in (2.5 mm) with $\frac{1}{16}$ in (1.5 mm) internal shelves and $\frac{1}{8}$ in (3 mm) square shelf supports.

If you are making an old-fashioned shop, you can find ideas from old photographs, showing everything piled high, inside and out.

If you wish to hang the shop on the wall, fix mirror plates on the back (Fig 188).

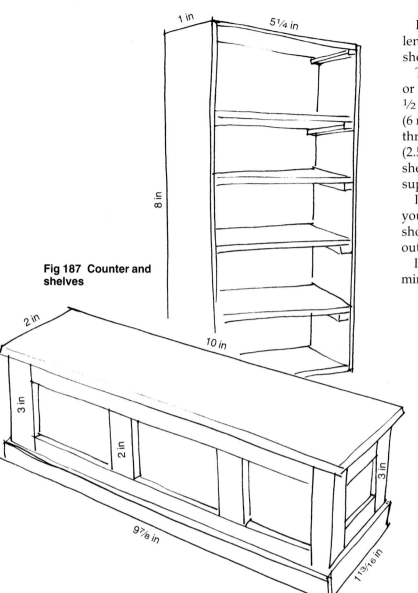

Fig 187 Counter and shelves

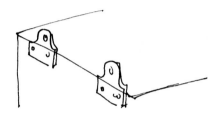

Fig 188 Mirror plates

LIGHTING

There are now some very realistic doll's house lights available, which can really transform a room.

The electric current is carried round the house by fine 2 mm twin-flex wire or two flat strips of adhesive copper tape, or a combination of both methods. Most collectors use 12 volt lights, run off a transformer which cuts down the mains supply from 240 volts in the UK or 120 volts in USA, so, although the lights are interchangeable, the transformers are not.

The type of transformer used depends on the number of bulbs (not just the light fittings). Each 12 volt bulb is rated between 40 and 60 milliamps, and a standard doll's house transformer of 1 amp/12 watts will take 1000 milliamps – about 20 bulbs. For more lights, use a 2 amp/20 watt transformer or two of 1 amp.

A smaller house with six to ten bulbs can use a ½ amp/5 watt transformer. A small transformer rated at 300 mA, sold in chainstores for use with radios and calculators, is ideal for a box room or shop with one or two lights.

A heavy-duty transformer will not damage a single bulb when testing, but prolonged use will burn out the bulb.

Most of these transformers are combined with the 13 amp plug. Those sold for model railways and racing cars are not recommended, as they have a variable current which could burn out the bulbs. I used a battery charger successfully for four years to light a model of Gainsborough's house.

The wires can be concealed by grooving the walls or ceilings, and covering with wallpaper or thin slivers of wood. If you drill a hole through the floor to hang a central light below, the floor will have to be covered with a (preferably removable) layer of wood flooring, or carpeted.

Wire can be added to an already decorated doll's house by running it along the cornices and top of skirtings, where an extra line will hardly show, just as many real electricians do. A straight line of wire back from a ceiling light will hardly show; use instant glue, or cover it with a thin strip of tape and paint white. (Masking tape and sellotape dry out, so you should use a stronger product from a DIY shop – white carpet tape, Scotch magic tape or mylar.)

Copper tape can be concealed under wallpaper and picked up with small brads, or pins, once you have decided where to put your lights. A small two-pronged probe which lights up when it makes contact is invaluable for checking where the tapes are, and testing for shorts.

The SIX-ROOM HOUSE is wired with a combination of wire and copper tape. The wire from each light is run through the back and soldered to strips of tape, which then connect to the transformer. The wires run along grooves in the ceilings and walls. The side lights share a channel behind the chimney breast, and the landing lights are wired up through the doorways and behind the skirting to the back (Fig 189).

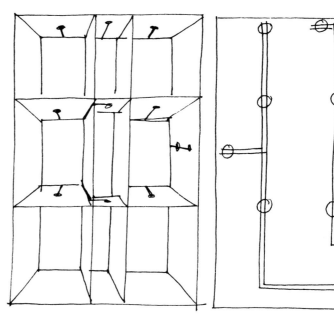

Fig 189 Lighting plan

Fig 190 Tape wiring plan

Fig 191 Turn double tape

Fig 192 Correct cross over joint, and two incorrect

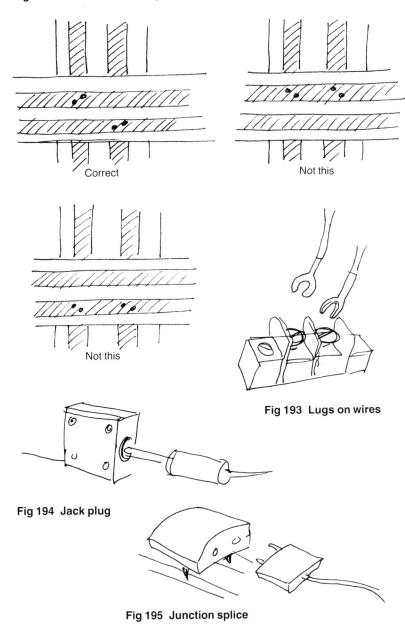

Correct

Not this

Not this

Fig 193 Lugs on wires

Fig 194 Jack plug

Fig 195 Junction splice

The holes and grooves should all be drilled and cut before the house is assembled, and recesses drilled in the back for spare wire at the junctions with the tape. (Alternatively, protective battens can be added later.)

Start by running double strips of tape down the back, over the recesses (Fig 190) and join near the bottom, to finish with a connector for the transformer. Make a right-angle turn by turning in the *opposite* direction, then fold back the correct way (Fig 191). Single tape should be rubbed down hard at the turn; double tape should be held down with a clear adhesive tape. Where the two double strips meet, they should join as illustrated (Fig 192) using brads.

Remember that one side is positive, the other negative, and that the two currents must be kept separate. If you are using single tape, use clear tape or white insulating tape where one crosses another. Solder single tape, or use 1/8 in (3 mm) brads. It is easier to pin double tape: you have to cut away the insulation when soldering.

There are various ways of fixing an outlet for the transformer. You can solder the wires to the tape and wrap them round two screws embedded into the wood. A similar fitting has two prongs which pierce the tape; the leads from the transformer are wound round the screws and screwed tight. (The wires *must* wind the same way that the screw tightens.) A tidier fitting is made by joining lugs to each wire and screwing them down (Fig 193). If the two live wires touch, they will short out the transformer, so always remember to switch it off before touching the wires. Most transformers have a trip switch, and if there is a short-circuit the transformer will cut out for half an hour. An easy connection is made with a spring-fitting resembling two light switches – press each switch to insert or release the wire. A jackplug makes a solid fitting, if you can find a simple one that takes two wires. If there is not enough wood to recess the socket in the side, fit a block on the back to take it (Fig 194). The neatest solution is a small junction splice, a 3/4 in (19 mm) square of plastic with brads that pin into the tape, and a small 6 mm plug (Fig 195).

Check that the tapes are conducting correctly with a probe or the two wires on a bulb, then solder the lights to the tapes, checking each one before and after fitting (but do *not* leave the transformer plugged in while you are working).

If you are using a plaster ceiling rose, thread the wire through from the light before gluing it to the ceiling. An instant glue makes a good bond which is easily broken when necessary with a sharp knife blade, and can be used on the ceiling fittings supplied in place of the adhesive pad.

Press the wire into the groove, and retain with a strip of wood to fit. Alternatively, cover with wallpaper or sticky tape. Feed the wire through the hole in the back. Leave slack both ends so that the wire can be pulled back and forth to avoid being glued. Alternatively, make a wider channel, push a stiffer wire through, and attach lighting wire by twisting or soldering and pulling through the back.

Once the wires are through, cut them short to 4 in (10 cm), split the ends and remove ¼ in (6 mm) insulation – using your finger-nail is easiest. Place 1/16 in (1.5 mm) wire core solder on the tape, add wire and heat with a soldering iron (25-30 volt pencil tip) until the solder melts into the wires (Fig 196). Solder each wire to a different tape, and check that the light works before gluing it in place and drawing through the slack wire, which is coiled in the recess and held with adhesive tape (Fig 197). Joints can be protected with clear tape and the whole back covered with a ⅛ in (3 mm) sheet of plywood. Cut away the section for the connector, and take care not to screw through the wiring.

If you cannot cut recesses, ⅛ in (3 mm) battens will hold the backing off the joins.

You could simply cover the bare copper tapes with strong transparent tape, or a white tape from a DIY store. Seal first with varnish and take care that the extra-sticky tape will not damage the wiring when removed. If you use the mylar-covered double tape, as long as the joints are protected with strong clear (or translucent Scotch) tape, no more covering is really needed.

Choose lights that have screw-in bulbs. Loosen them before fitting, as sometimes the glue from the shade has spread. To remove a bulb once a light is fitted, wrap a little sellotape or masking tape round the bulb to turn it.

If you have to change a grain-of-wheat bulb, soldered to two wires, you will have to solder the ends to the existing wires and pull them through to the back. Cut the ceiling wire, remove the rose, feed the new wire through the light and rose, then solder to the end of the ceiling wire, where the 4 in (10 cm) slack is necessary. If the new wire will reach the joint, it does not matter how you solder the lead wire. If, however, you need a join in the recessed channel, a staggered joint will have to be made. Join the wires 1 in (2.5 cm) apart and insulate with glue or a special shrink tube, if available. This fits over one strand of wire and shrinks to fit when heated (Fig 198).

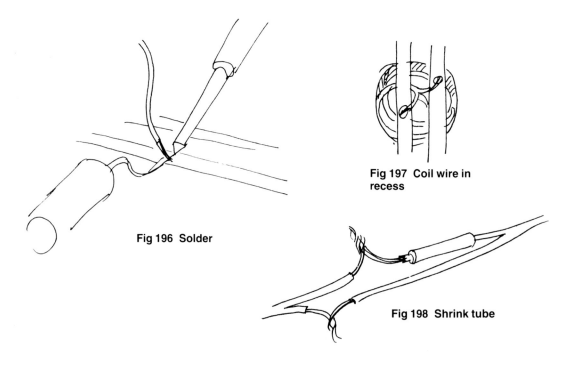

Fig 196 Solder

Fig 197 Coil wire in recess

Fig 198 Shrink tube

Choose your lighting to suit the rooms – simple overhead lights, a grand chandelier or a bedside lamp

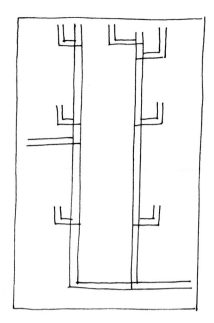

Fig 199 Double tape
wiring plan

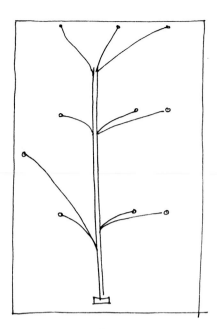

Fig 200 Round wire
plan

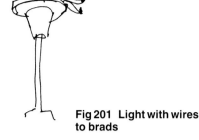

Fig 201 Light with wires
to brads

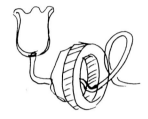

Fig 202 Wall light and
spacer

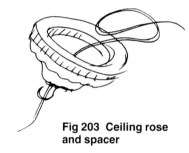

Fig 203 Ceiling rose
and spacer

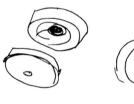

Fig 204 Plastic screw
covers

Fig 205 Two-part
canopy

If you use tape throughout, you can use a similar pattern of wiring (Fig 199), but remember to run the tapes off-centre to allow for right-angled joints. It is possible to make an almost continuous strip of tape round the house by folding across ceilings and round doorways to avoid too many joins, but I prefer to drill a few holes and have accessible joins rather than feed long lengths of tape through cracks and disguise bumps on the ceiling. If you are using single tape, protect with clear tape or varnish before painting over it, as the surface tends to oxidize.

If you are using wire throughout, choose a thicker wire, 22 gauge, which can carry up to 2 amp as the 'feed' wire. The fine wire used for the lights will only carry about six 12 volt bulbs (Fig 200).

If you do not want to have to remove the back of the house every time a bulb needs changing, you can attach the lights inside but they may not look as neat.

Most lights come with a plug attached but this, added to a wall socket, can be rather unsightly. You may be able to recess the socket into the wall, attached to tape or wire, and hide it behind a chimney breast or piece of furniture. Alternatively, insert eyelets in the copper tape to fit the plug, or attach the wires to brads and pin them to the tape. A wire-to-wire joint, well insulated, can be concealed in a corner.

The main problem is that light fittings have a solid base and no room to hide the slack wire needed when you make a joint. Some lights are glued to the ceiling, with their wires tied or soldered to brads just out of sight behind the fittings (Fig 201), but this leaves no spare wire. If you make a hollow spacer between the ceilings or wall and the light (Fig 202), or behind a ceiling rose (Fig 203), this will take spare wire. You could use a plastic screw cover to hide the brads or wire joints (Fig 204). There is an excellent two-part ceiling fitting available which pins to tape or can be attached to wires; the canopy removes so that the light can be attached (Fig 205). Ceiling roses are now available with prongs to fit brads in the tape; you can also buy a smaller back plate for use with wall lights. They are easy to remove, and the lighting wires attach to the prongs.

Toy shops usually stock lower-voltage 3 volt lights which can only be run off 3 volt transformers. A higher voltage will blow the bulbs. You can change the bulbs to 12V if you wish to use a 12V system, but take care that the hotter bulb will not damage the lights. The plugs on these lights have slightly thicker prongs than the 12V so are not inter-changeable. Some lighting sets contain a bar of sockets which should be hidden on the back, creating the problem of drilling for wires, removing plugs, then replacing them. It is much simpler to join the lights to a thicker 2 amp wire. You can use plastic connectors if you are joining a few wires, or solder them to the wire and insulate (Fig 206).

If you are using lights with a threaded brass holder, solder one wire to the side and the other to the insulated base (Fig 207). The 1.5V bulbs will only run off a battery.

If you wish to light an antique doll's house, do not damage the fabric of the house. Concealed lighting hidden behind a batten at ceiling height, or even fixed to the opening front, works better than introducing a modern light. Flora Gill Jacob's doll's houses in the Washington Doll's House and Toy Museum are lit in this way.

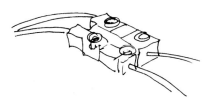

Fig 206 Junction block

Fig 207 1.5 volt bulb

CONCLUSION

Now that you have seen how one basic design can be adapted, I hope you will be inspired to make some variations of your own.

Go out with a camera and photograph houses that appeal to you. I know some Belgians who did just that when they were planning a full-size château, and built their dream home, but when the Second World War came they lost it for ever. If it had been a doll's house, they might have been able to remove it to safety!

An American customer who had spent some very happy years in a Tudor house in East Anglia ordered a Tudor doll's house to be sent to her and furnished it in replica, complete with framed photographs of her husband's collection of paintings.

An early Victorian detached London house; eighteenth-century Essex weatherboard, with a tiled roof, sash windows, and additional porch; weathered thatch, with 'stitched' ridge, and bargeboards

Georgian door and fanlight; seventeenth or eighteenth-century cottage door and window, single opening casement window, random Cotswold stone, and graduated stone roof; front door in a Victorian terrace of artisans' houses; modern glazed door and Georgian style surround; Victorian cottage door, with rainstrip along the bottom, double casement windows, arched brickwork, and tar waterproofing along the foot of the wall; sash windows in a Victorian house of coursed Cotswold stone, with glazed top door panels

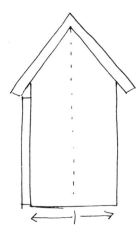

Fig 208 Incorrect overhang

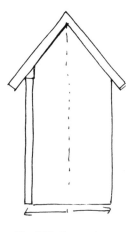

Fig 209 Correct overhang

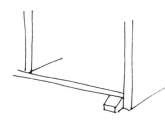

Fig 210 Block to support Front

There are some important points to remember. If you build a house with the Back fitted between the Sides, remember to cut the apex of the Side Wall off-centre (Fig 208). Most people forget that the overall depth includes the opening Front, and perhaps ⅛ in (3 mm) for the hinge. If the apex is centred, the Front will come out too far, leaving a correct roof overhang at the back and none at the front (Fig 209).

If you do not want any pavement under the Front, this must still be able to swing clear of the ground (as in the BOX SHOP). A small block of ⅜ in (9 mm) can be pinned and glued under the Base next to the opening, extending ⅜ in (9 mm) – the depth of the Front – from the main body of the house (Fig 210). This will stop the Front dropping away from the hinges. A six-room house may need two hook eyes or magnet catches to keep the Front closed flat.

Before cutting windows in the Front, check where they look best by using panels of coloured paper cut to size. You can see then the pattern they make, whether they need to be closer to the roof, etc.

If you want to renovate an old doll's house, check what scale it is. If it is a smaller scale, ¾ in : 1 ft (¹⁄₁₆th scale), with doorways about 4 in (10.2 cm) high and 5 in (12.7 cm) ceilings, you will only be able to furnish it with the smaller mass-produced furniture available in toy shops, unless you make your own.

Any house made pre-First World War tends to be classified as antique (even though not 100 years old), and should be treated with respect. It should be conserved but not over-restored. The well-known collector Vivien Greene, who started collecting in 1944, before anyone else, discovered an unusual early nineteenth-century doll's house and asked if she could bring a group of collectors back to see it. When she returned some weeks later, the proud owner had re-decorated it in their honour, complete with green baize carpet. All the original weathered paint had gone, and it might just as well have been a modern replica.

So I suggest you keep the fine detail for your new doll's houses, and leave antique ones in their crude original state. If you need to remove newer paint, try to flake it off with your fingernail; even a blunt knife can chip the paint beneath. A purist, like Faith Eaton, (collector, conservator and author) will only redecorate her doll's houses with wallpaper of the correct decade (many remain bare!) and antique doll's house furniture. Personally, I find some of the cruder Taiwan furniture will fit in an antique doll's house, and this means it can actually be furnished and 'lived' in.

I have enjoyed planning this book. Each doll's house took on a different character as it was furnished – the simple Taiwan furniture in the BASIC HOUSE, with the mothers drinking orange juice in the kitchen, the Victorian family in the BRICK HOUSE, (mostly Taiwan furniture) the rather 'green' family in the WEATHERBOARD HOUSE, who like stripped pine and primitive paintings (all handmade) and the Victorian family in the FLINT HOUSE, which has a well-blended mix of Taiwan and handmade furniture. The TUDOR HOUSE has seventeenth-century oak furniture, but could be lived in by an antique collector of any later date. The SIX-ROOM HOUSE is very 'Upstairs-Downstairs', with its plump cook, maid and nanny, and a very elegant family and handmade furniture. The BOX SHOP took even longer to fit out with all its hardware, groceries and rather crusty shopkeeper.

I hope you will have equal enjoyment when planning your doll's house and I look forward to seeing some of the results.

GLOSSARY

anaglypta embossed wallpaper used for ceilings; a smaller pattern was also used as a dado (up to chair-rail height) to protect the walls of a staircase or a corridor

architrave moulding surrounding a doorway or window

astragal rounded, almost cylindrical, moulding

balusters short bottle-shaped supports for parapet; another name for banisters

bargeboard wooden strip protecting timbers at the gable end of a roof

beam horizontal timber supporting floor joists or rafters

bevel reduce a right angle to a slope

capital section at the top of a pillar

casement window hinged like a door; English windows open outwards, with indoor shutters; Continental ones open inwards, with exterior shutters

chamfer round off a sharp edge

chimney breast brick fireplace surround extending into the room (otherwise the chimney is contained within the thickness of the wall, or added to the exterior)

coping protective strip of stonework on top of a sloping wall

cornice moulding at the join between wall and ceiling, or along the top of a wall

dentil strip of moulding resembling a row of cubes, used below a cornice

door jamb upright post supporting doorway

dowel round wooden rod

eaves underneath section of overhanging roof

eyelets tubular brass pins used for joining copper tape for lighting; the larger ones are used as sockets for electric plugs

fanlight glazed opening above front door, originally fan-shaped

finial decorative addition to the top of a gable, often ending in a ball or spike (the one on the Flint House porch could extend upwards)

firebasket free standing cast iron grate

fire dogs a pair of cast iron uprights (to stop the logs rolling forward) each supported by a bracket on which the logs rest

flagstones large slabs of stone used for flooring or pavements

gable end the triangular topped end wall below a ridged roof

glazing bars these hold the panes of glass

Georgian 1714-1830

halving joint cut-away half of each surface to be joined

hearthstone Victorian method of whitening steps; a block of hearthstone was rubbed into the dampened surface

hinge, butt flat, the sides touch when closed

hinge, cranked bent at a right angle to fit round the side of the panel

hinge, piano long strip, used on piano lids

inglenook large opening for fire, which burns on the open hearth; usually large enough to sit in

keystone central stone, usually of an arch

leaded window small panes were set in strips of lead, before large sheets of glass were available

leads lengths of wire

lintel wood or stone support across the top of a door or window

mirror plate flat brass plate screwed to the back of a mirror, the projecting portion fixes to the wall; a variable hole will allow for lifting off

mitre corner joint cut at a right angle

mortar sand mixed with cement or lime

mouldings shaped strips of wood of uniform cross-section

newel post support at top and bottom of banisters

pediment triangular shape above doorway or window

picture rail small strip of moulding a few feet below a tall ceiling from which pictures are suspended on chains or cord

Plasticine malleable substance used by children for modelling (non-hardening clay)

quoins corner-stones of a building

rail, bottom strip supporting the base of the banisters

rainstrip projection to deflect rain above a window, or along the bottom of a door

Regency 1811-1820

retainer an overlapping strip to hold glazing etc in place

riser the upright part of a step

rustication stonework with chamfered joints

sash window slides up and down in grooves, balanced by weights

skirting board along the bottom of an interior wall

spacer wood cut to length to keep panels correct distance apart while assembling

string strip along the edge of a staircase

stucco plaster facing on a wall

studs upright timbers constructing a wall

trapdoor hinged opening to loft

tread flat part of step

Tudor 1485-1603

Victorian 1837—1901

window sill projecting slab of wood or stone at the base of a window

PUBLICATIONS & FAIRS

Magazines

International Dolls' House News
PO Box 79
Southampton SO9 7EZ
(Established 1967. Quarterly.)

Dolls' House World
Ashdown Publications
Shelley House
104 High Street
Steyning
Sussex BN44 3RD
(Established 1989. Bi-monthly.)

The Home Miniaturist
Ashdown Publications
(see above)
(Established 1979. Bi-monthly.)

Dolls House and Miniature Scene
5 Cissbury Road
Ferring
West Sussex BN12 6QJ
(Established 1992. Bi-monthly.)

The Miniature Gazette
National Association of Miniature
Enthusiasts (N.A.M.E.)
PO Box 69
Carmel
IN 46032
(Established 1974. Quarterly.)

Nutshell News
Kalmbach Publishing Co.
PO Box 1612
Waukeshka
WI 53187
USA
(Established 1970. Monthly.)

Books

*Nora Earnshaw, *Collecting Dolls' Houses and Miniatures*, Collins

*Faith Eaton, *The Miniature House*, Weidenfeld and Nicolson

Caroline Hamilton, *Decorative Dolls' Houses*, Ebury Press

Jessica Ridley, *The Decorated Doll's House*, Macdonald

Barbara Warner, *Dollhouse Lighting*, Boynton

You can also find inspiration from books and magazines on full-size houses and interior decoration.

*Mostly concerned with antique doll's houses, and shows authentic miniature interiors.

Fairs

The London Dollshouse Festival
Kensington Town Hall
London W8
May
(all enquiries to:
25 Priory Road
Kew Green
Richmond
Surrey TW9 3DQ)

Miniatura
National Exhibition Centre
Birmingham
March and September
(all enquiries to:
41 Eastbourne Avenue
Hodge Hill
Birmingham B34 6AR)

A comprehensive list of shops, fairs and suppliers is published in the *London Dollshouse Festival Hobby Directory*, available from 25 Priory Road, Kew Green, Richmond, Surrey TW9 3DQ. The Doll's House Information Service, Ash Grove, Cross-in-Hand, Heathfield, Sussex and the specialist magazines also supply details. Enclose a stamped addressed envelope or international reply coupon to ensure a reply.

SUPPLIERS

Specialist shops (UK)

The Dolls House
29 The Market
Covent Garden
London WC2E 8RE
Tel: 071-379 7243
(Established in 1971 by Michal Morse)

The China Doll
32 Walcot Street
Bath
Avon
Tel: 0225 65849

Dorking Dolls' House Gallery
23 West Street
Dorking
Surrey RH4 1BY
Tel: 0306 885785

Fiddly Bits
24 King Street
Knutsford
Cheshire WA16 6DW
Tel: 0565 51119

Royal Mile Miniatures
154 Cannongate
Royal Mile
Edinburgh EH8 8DD
Tel: 031-557 2293

Wansbeck Hobbies
2 Chapel Yard
Holt
Norfolk NR25 6HX
Tel: 0263 713933

Specialist shops (USA)

Angel's Attic
516 Colorado Avenue
Santa Monica
CA 90401
Tel: (213) 394 8331

Little Things
129 Main Street
Irvington
NY 10533
Tel: (914) 591 9150

Mary Merritt Doll Museum
Rt 422
Douglasville
PA 19518
Tel: (215) 385 3809

Miniature Mart
1807 Octavia Street
San Francisco
CA 94109
Tel: (417) 563 7436
(Mail order, or appointment)

Washington Doll's House & Toy Museum
Museum Shop
5236 44th Street NW
Washington
DC 20015
Tel: (202) 244 0024

Modellers' timber and tools

Borcraft Miniatures
8 Fairfax View
Scotland Lane
Horsforth
Leeds
West Yorkshire LS18 5SZ
Tel: 0532 588 739

W. Hobby Ltd
Knights Hill Square
London SE27 0HH
Tel: 081-761 4244

Blackwells of Hawkwell
733 London Road
Westcliff-on-Sea
Essex SS0 9ST
Tel: 0702 72248

And so to bed . . .

INDEX